THE WORLD OF
· COCKATOOS ·

THE WORLD OF
COCKATOOS

Karl Diefenbach

**translated by
Annemarie Lambrich**

Frontispiece: Lesser Sulphur-crested Cockatoo (*C. s. citrinocristata*).

Photographs: Thomas Brosset, Karl Diefenbach (from the collection of Alfons Preussiger, Neuwied), Angelika Fergenbauer-Kimmel, Hermann Fritsch, Wolfgang de Grahl, Dr. Klaus Immelmann, Povl Jorgensen, Winfried Krause, Heinz Leibfarth, Dr. P. E. Roders, Josef Schumacher, Karl W. Steinert, Thomas Weise, Tierpark Gettorf, Vogelpark Walsrode/Müller.

Drawings: Ursula Wedde, Waiblingen.

Cages and stands: Wagner & Keller, Ludwigsburg.

Photographs added to the English-language edition: Dr. Gerald R. Allen, 150 bottom. Glen S. Axelrod, 75 bottom, 127 bottom. Dr. Herbert R. Axelrod, 127 top. Thomas Brosset, 103. Kerry V. Donnelly, 66. M. Guevara, 79. Fred Harris, 135. Keith Hindwood, 67 bottom. Ralph Kaehler, frontis, 19, 43, 74, 158, 159. Don Mathews, 14, 15. Stefan Norberg & Anders Hansson, 7. Louise Van der Meid, 11.

Distributed in the UNITED STATES by T.F.H. Publications, Inc., 211 West Sylvania Avenue, Neptune City, NJ 07753; in CANADA by H & L Pet Supplies Inc., 27 Kingston Crescent, Kitchener, Ontario N2B 2T6; rolf C. Hagen Ltd., 3225 Sartelon Street, Montreal 382 Quebec; in ENGLAND by T.F.H. Publications Limited, 4 Kier Park, Ascot, Berkshire SL5 7DS; in AUSTRALIA AND THE SOUTH PACIFIC by T.F.H. (Australia) Pty. Ltd., Box 149, Brookvale 2100 N.S.W., Australia; in NEW ZEALAND by Ross Haines & Son, Ltd., 18 Monmouth Street, Grey Lynn, Auckland 2 New Zealand; in SINGAPORE AND MALAYSIA by MPH Distributors Pte., 71-77 Stamford Road, Singapore 0617; in the PHILIPPINES by Bio-Research, 5 Lippay Street, San Lorenzo Village, Makati Rizal; in SOUTH AFRICA by Multipet Pty. Ltd., 30 Turners Avenue, Durban 4001. Published by T.F.H. Publications Inc., Ltd. the British Crown Colony of Hong Kong.

Contents

Introduction 8

Systematic Status 12
Anatomy: Skeleton — Musculature —
Digestive Organs — Plumage —
Development of the Young — Feather Lice
— Behavior — How to Recognize a
Cockatoo

Cockatoo Behavior 29
Field Observations — Maintenance Activi-
ties — Locomotion — Feeding — Resting
and Sleeping — Temperature Regulation —
Comfort Behavior — Grooming — Stretch-
ing — Bathing — Scratching — Social
Behavior — Social Feather Grooming —
Mate Feeding — Agonistic Behavior —
Reproductive Behavior

Purchase and Acclimation 48

Accommodations 52
Cages — Stands, Bow Perches, Climbing
Trees — Room Aviaries — Flight Rooms —
Outdoor Aviaries

Nutrition 60
The Diet of Wild Cockatoos — Nutrition in
Captivity: Seed — Sprouts — Green Foods
— Fruits, Vegetables, Berries — Foods of
Animal Origin — Minerals — Vitamins —
Rearing Foods

Care 68
Grooming and Feather Trimming —
Trimming the Claws and Beak —
Temperature and Humidity — Hygiene —
Illness — Taming

Breeding 76
Preparations — Nest Boxes and Material —
Breeding and Rearing — Artificial Rearing

Species Accounts 85
Genus *PROBOSCIGER*, 85
Palm Cockatoo, 85
Genus *CALYPTORHYNCHUS*, 90
Black Cockatoo, 90
Red-tailed Cockatoo, 94
Glossy Cockatoo, 99
Genus *CALLOCEPHALON*, 101
Gang-gang Cockatoo, 101
Genus *EOLOPHUS*, 105
Galah, 105
Genus *CACATUA*, 110
Major Mitchell's Cockatoo, 111
Lesser Sulphur-crested Cockatoo, 114
Sulphur-crested Cockatoo, 118
Blue-eyed Cockatoo, 123
Salmon-crested Cockatoo, 124
White Cockatoo, 128
Red-vented Cockatoo, 132
Goffin's Cockatoo, 134
Little Corella, 137
Long-billed Corella, 141
Ducorps's Cockatoo, 144
Genus *NYMPHICUS*, 145
Cockatiel, 145

Bibliography 153

Indexes 156

The bright red cheek patches show that this
pair of Palm Cockatoos (*P. a. goliath*) are in
excellent health.

**Sulphur-crested Cockatoo (*C. g. galerita*),
female, 7 years old.**

Introduction

Ranging in length from thirty to seventy cm., cockatoos are among the largest Old World parrots. The distribution of the six genera—a total of eighteen species—extends from the Philippines to Australia and Tasmania. There probably is no other group of parrots as characteristic of this continent as the cockatoos; eleven species occur here alone. On the various islands —namely, besides the Philippines, the islands of the Bismarck Archipelago, the Solomons, Celebes, the Lesser Sunda Islands (Lombok, Sumbawa, Sumba, Flores, and Timor), the islands of the Moluccan group, and New Guinea—no more than one or two species are found. Cockatoos have always been welcome pets, and this is true not only for the natives in their home range; a long time ago they were brought to Europe by sailors returning from their travels and enjoyed great popularity, then as now, as cage and aviary birds. Once well-acclimated, most species are not difficult to care for and go on to breed relatively easily. As talkers, cockatoos are not comparable to Grey Parrots or amazons, but they distinguish themselves by taming easily and by their affection toward their keepers. However, there is no joking with the strong beak of a cockatoo; the name *cockatoo* is derived from a Malay word that means "pincer."

This book is intended as a guide for the cockatoo fancier, and the cockatoo breeder in particular. Special attention is devoted to cockatoo behavior, since an awareness of this will provide important insights into the psyches of one's charges and, among other things, will prove valuable in breeding them. It must be emphasized here that cockatoos should be kept in pairs, because the only valid rationale that can be brought forward for the importation of some species is attempting to breed them. Because of changes in their environment and the destruction of their natural habitat, many parrot populations have been extensively reduced; cockatoos especially have been struck by the aimless deforestation of their home ranges. Because of constant global population growth, virgin forests and uninhabited regions give way to cultivation; where a nesting tree used to stand, a derrick now rises toward the sky. Species endemic to small islands deserve our special protection since there is no hinterland, should they be decimated by intensive capture or habitat destruction, in which to regenerate.

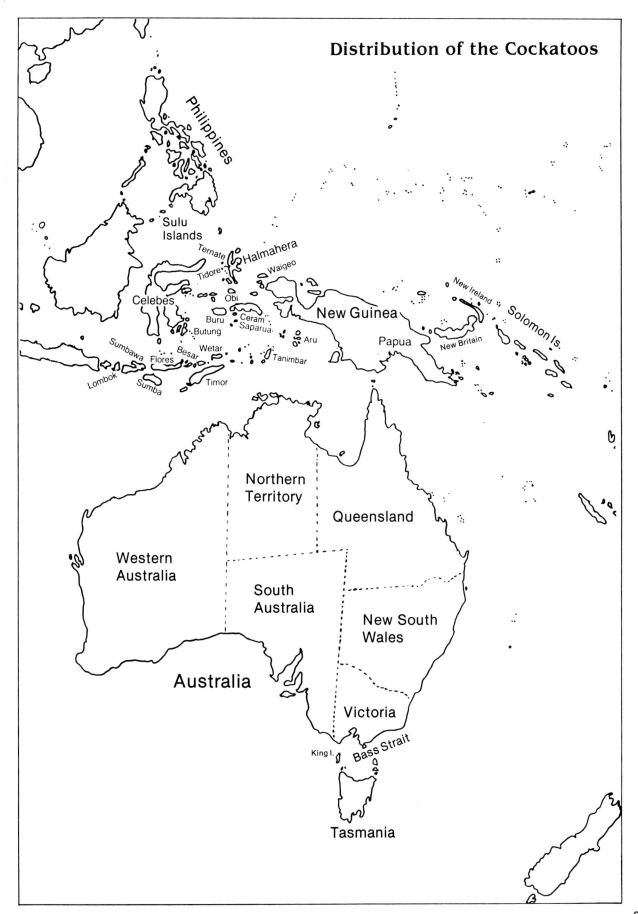

Distribution of the Cockatoos

Philippines

Sulu
Islands

Ternate Halmahera

Tidore Waigeo

Celebes Obi

Buru Ceram
Saparua

Butung

New Guinea

New Ireland Solomon Is.

Papua New Britain

Sumbawa Besar Wetar

Flores Tanimbar

Lombok Aru

Sumba Timor

Northern
Territory

Queensland

Western
Australia

South
Australia

New South
Wales

Australia

Victoria

Bass Strait

King I.

Tasmania

Above: Dry riverbed in the desert region of central Australia. In the tall eucalyptus trees, nesting cavities of Galahs (*E. r. roseicapillus*), Major Mitchell's (*C. l. leadbeateri*), and Red-tailed (*C. m. samueli*) cockatoos can be found.
Left: Sulphur-crested Cockatoo (*C. g. triton*), male.

Galahs (*E. roseicapillus*).

Systematic Status

Systematics, or taxonomy, is not only an important subdiscipline of ornithology, but of biology in general. It concerns itself with the kinship relations of all living things and attempts to organize them hierarchically. Closely associated is scientific nomenclature, which since Linnaeus has employed predominantly Latin and Greek words; in this way, it guarantees international communication.

The basic unit of systematics is the species; this encompasses all those organisms that conform in all essential characteristics and constitute a reproductive community. The next higher unit, the genus, includes several species; several genera form a family, several families form an order; several orders a class. The class of vertebrates called birds (Aves) should be mentioned here as an example. If the categories named are inadequate, intermediate categories such as subfamily, subspecies, etc., are added; within one species there may be different subspecies and geographic races.

The parrots form their own, distinctly separable order which is clearly defined on the basis of numerous characteristics. Anatomical characteristics, ontogenesis (development of the individual), occurrence of Mallophaga (feather lice), and behavior are factors used in the determination of their systematic placement. In addition, serological tests and analyses of the composition of egg-white proteins have been used successfully for more than a decade to review various families, genera, and species.

Anatomy: Skeleton The skeleton of a bird is characterized by its light weight; this is the result of pneumatization of many bones, the reduction of unnecessary parts, and the transformation of massive parts into thin-shell constructions (e.g., the pelvis). Compared with the skeletons of other birds, that of the parrot shows the following characteristics, some typical: Parrots are—with the exception of the Night Parrot *(Geopsittacus occidentalis)* and the Kakapo *(Strigops habroptilus)*—arboreal birds; feet suited to climbing and a short gait are indications of this way of life. The zygodactyl position of the toes make the parrot foot an excellent gripping tool; the first and fourth toes point to the back, the second and third to the front. This pattern is typical of other tree-dwelling bird species also: woodpeckers, toucans, and cuckoos, for example.

Another important parrot characteristic is the powerful, strongly curved upper mandible, which is movably attached to the brain case—a great advantage in picking up and chewing food, as well as in climbing. The bonelike beak, like the claws, is covered with a horny substance which is continually renewed by blood-carrying tissue. In this manner, the horny parts grow constantly; under normal conditions this keeps pace with the constant wear. In captivity, disturbances of this equilibrium are apt to occur and may necessitate trimming the claws and beak. At its base the beak is surrounded by the cere, which may be naked or feathered, depending on the species; in it are the two nostrils, the only openings in the completely fused boney substrate of the upper mandible. In most parrot species, horny crisscross ridges ("file grooves") are found on the inside of the upper mandible and perform two important functions. They sharpen the edge of the lower mandible, and they also play an important part in holding and breaking up solid food particles; consequently, they are especially well developed in seed- and nut-eaters. The size and shape of the beak are closely related to body size, as well as to the principal type of food. For instance, the upper

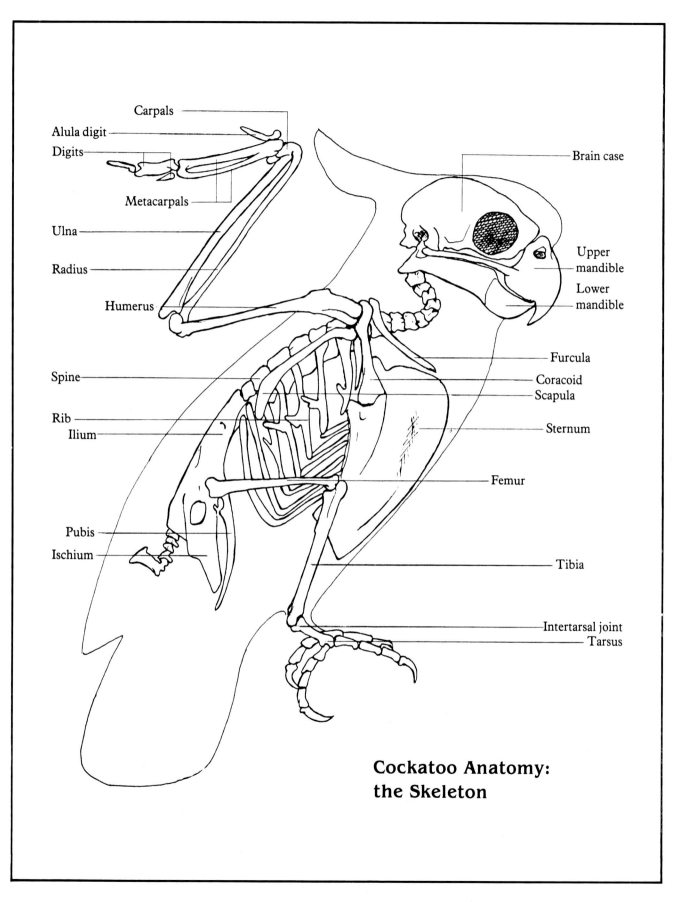

Carpals

Alula digit

Digits

Metacarpals

Ulna

Radius

Humerus

Spine

Rib

Ilium

Pubis

Ischium

Brain case

Upper mandible

Lower mandible

Furcula

Coracoid

Scapula

Sternum

Femur

Tibia

Intertarsal joint

Tarsus

**Cockatoo Anatomy:
the Skeleton**

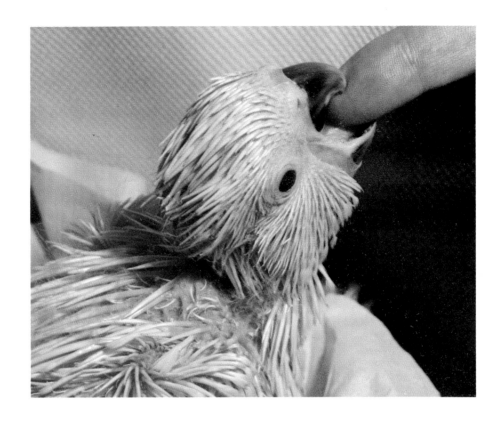

Lesser Sulphur-crested Cockatoo (*C. s. citrinocristata*), 38 days old (above) and 42 days old (below).

Lesser Sulphur-crested Cockatoo (*C. s. citrinocristata*), 8 weeks old (above) and 10 weeks old (below).

mandible of the Long-billed Corella *(C. tenuirostris)* is especially long and excellently suited for digging in the ground for sprouting seeds; conversely, parrots that feed predominantly on pollen, nectar, and fruit have a comparatively small beak.

The brain case itself is rounded; in cockatoos the lacrimal and temporal bones are connected by a narrow band of bone, forming a complete ring around the eye socket.

Musculature   The arrangement and proportions of certain muscles have a special taxonomic importance in determining the systematization of the various groups of birds. The thigh muscles, for which the arrangement can vary greatly, are a good example. All the muscles in the thigh and pelvic area are well developed and connected to the skeletal parts of foot and leg with long tendons; this explains the great strength of the parrot foot. The tendon that closes the foot can be held fast by a locking mechanism so that constant muscle tension is unnecessary; this has special significance for tree-roosting parrots. The beak musculature of all species also is well developed.

Digestive Organs   The tongues of parrots vary from the pestle tongues of the seed eaters to the papilla-covered brushlike tongues of the nectar feeders. As a muscular and richly innervated organ, in all instances it has important functions in feeding, but not in vocalizations, as was assumed in the past. In seed-eating species, the system of tongue and upper and lower mandibles works to hull and break up seeds; this applies to the tongue of the cockatoo, which is furnished with structures capable of swelling. The spindle-shaped or sac-like crop is an enlargement of the esophagus and in parrots has two important roles: One is to store and soak food, which is released in portions to the stomach. It is also capable of "antiperistalsis," i.e., food can be regurgitated for feeding the mate or the young. While in finches the crop begins to fill only after the stomach is already full, in all parrots the crop will remain full for some time even if the stomach is empty. Certain enzymes are added here to prepare the food for digestion. Whether some enzymes from the proventriculus also contribute to the steeping and digestive processes in the crop thus far has not been demonstrated for parrots with any certainty. Often one hears the assertion that, like pigeons, parrots produce in their crops a substance rich in protein and fat, the so-called crop milk, during the first days of rearing young. To date, however, this cannot be considered proven. The very presence of a crop has to be viewed in the light of adaptation to habitats in which food is not evenly distributed. Thus it is advantageous to the bird to take as much food as possible when it is at a feeding place. This sort of adaptation is known not only in seed eaters, but in extreme cases even in fish eaters.

The parrot stomach consists of two functionally separate parts, the proventriculus and the ventriculus. The first exhibits only a weak musculature; its main contribution is the production of digestive juices. The ventriculus is well developed, except in pollen- and nectar-eaters. Two pairs of muscles that grind down the food are distinctive. Swallowed gravel strengthens the rubbing and grinding effected by the ventriculus. The nutritional and physiological necessity for the ingestion of such material is obvious; therefore, sand and gravel should be made available to imported birds, especially those which have been kept in all-metal cages during quarantine. Since one usually does not know what the conditions during quarantine were like, this is particularly true for acclimating newly released birds. In fruit eaters, the ventriculus is a soft-skinned bag with a musculature greatly reduced due to its lack of function. The damage done, for instance, in "adapting" lories to seed will sooner or later lead to the death of the birds. The parts of the digestive tract are diversely developed, according to food specialization. Parrots lack caeca, which most birds have in pairs.

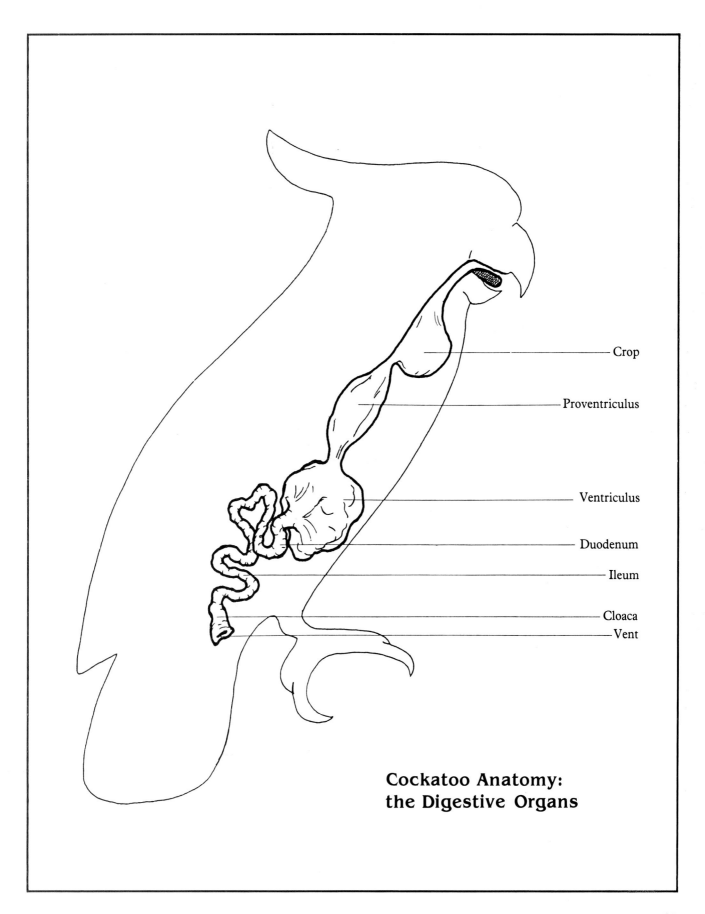

Crop

Proventriculus

Ventriculus

Duodenum

Ileum

Cloaca

Vent

**Cockatoo Anatomy:
the Digestive Organs**

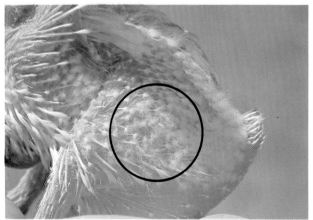

Above: Little Corellas (*C. s. sanguinea*) are elegant fliers, with good endurance. They will fly away, screeching loudly, at the slightest disturbance.
Left: Powder-down region on a young Little Corella (*C. s. sanguinea*).

White Cockatoo (*C. alba*), 47 days old, 350 grams.

Plumage The plumage of birds is an adaptation to flying, a way of life otherwise unknown in the animal kingdom. It also plays an important role in thermal insulation; because of the high body temperature of birds, this has a special significance. The fully grown bird feather is a structure of the epidermis. Feathers can be roughly classified as contour or down feathers. They are complexly constructed of a horny substance. The quill has an opening at the point where the main shaft and vane, and often an afterfeather, emerge. The main shaft (and the aftershaft) has barbs on each side which form the vane; the barbs in turn branch off into barbules. In contour, wing, and tail feathers, the barbules have tiny hooks which connect together to form the feather vanes. The down feathers lie under the contour feathers; since their only function is thermal insulation, the hooks are absent, and with them the solid vane.

The splendid color of parrots arises partly from material that is itself colored and partly from so-called structural colors. Among the actually colored materials are black and brown pigments, the melanins, and the fat-soluble red and yellow carotenoids. Structural colors, on the other hand, are due to the refraction of light. Thus white-colored plumage is caused by refracted light emerging from gas-filled cloudy cells of the feather barbs. If the red part of the spectrum is absorbed by a substrate of black melanin pigment, only the blue rays are reflected, resulting in blue-colored plumage. Green and violet are mixed colors, which are formed by yellow carotenoid and structural blue, and red carotenoid and structural blue, respectively.

The coloration and the markings of parrot plumage may vary depending on age and sex. If a species is sexually dimorphic, this is so throughout its life, instead of being restricted to the breeding season as in many other birds— weaver finches, for example. While most birds renew their plumage once or twice annually during a hormonally controlled molting period, parrots renew theirs continually; i.e., at all times their skin has new feathers in all stages of growth. However, a maximum can be observed after the end of a breeding period.

Contour feathers are situated only in the so-called feather tracts, between which are found numerous down feathers. The number of flight feathers in birds varies from group to group. For instance, there are species which lack the fifth secondary, even though the corresponding secondary coverts are present; this phenomenon, known as diastataxis, is found in parrots. The number of primaries varies only minimally within the class of birds; for parrots, having ten is characteristic. Much more pronounced from order to order are differences in the number of secondaries.

The skin itself is dry; skin glands are absent, except for the paired oil glands on the rump. In many parrots these are much reduced and practically without function; in some species, they are no longer present. The oil gland supplies oil for the plumage; in part its task is performed by powder downs. Many species of parrots have these down feathers: growing constantly, the barbs disintegrate into a powderlike

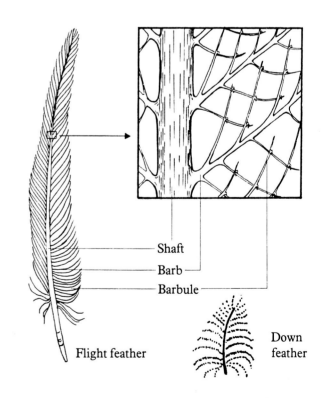

Shaft
Barb
Barbule

Flight feather

Down feather

dust, which is thoroughly distributed by ruffling the feathers and settles to protect the surfaces of the contour feathers. Like the oil of the rump glands, the oily feather powder is waterproof; it protects the plumage from becoming wet.

Legs and feet are covered by horny scales and plates, in an arrangement that may also be taxonomically significant. The age-dependent structural changes of the horny substance may be used as an indication of a parrot's age. Generally, it may be said that the thickness of the horny scales and their hardness increase with the age of the animal.

Development of the Young   Young parrots come into the world almost naked and very helpless. They must remain under the protection of their parents for a lengthy growing period; this necessitates intensive brood care. In ontogeny, such birds are said to be nidicolous. Since almost all parrots are cavity breeders—the exception of the Monk Parakeet *(Myiopsitta monachus)* may be mentioned in passing—neither ontogeny of this sort with its protracted postembryonic development nor the absence of camouflaging colors on the eggs constitutes an important selective disadvantage; protected by the nest cavity, eggs and nestlings are safe from most enemies.

Further, a long nestling period indicates a high degree of evolution in the class Aves. The duration of postembryonic development is species-characteristic and directly proportional to the body size of the species in question. The weight increases typical of nidicolous nestlings is illustrated here by the Cockatiel *(N. hollandicus)*. This curve shows a pronounced gain in weight by the nestling during the first twenty-four days of its life; initially quite considerable, it decreases later. After the twenty-fourth day weight gradually decreases again, until about the thirty-second day a value is attained that roughly approximates the average weight of an adult bird. At this point, the young are no longer fed so much. They leave the nest at thirty-three days.

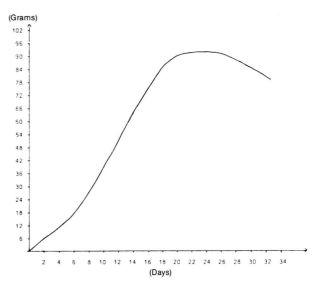

Weight Gain of a Cockatiel (*N. hollandicus*) Nestling.

Feather Lice   Besides physical and chemical (abiotic) factors, associations with other organisms (biotic factors) are part of the ecological conditions in which living creatures exist. The phenomenon of parasitism is one example. Because of the close ecological interrelations between parasite (e.g., feather louse, mite, etc.) and host (bird), this association is of special interest for the phyletic history of the species and therefore its systematic placement. The best-studied example involves Mallophaga (feather lice), which, as permanent ectoparasites, depend for dispersion on bodily contact of their hosts; consequently, they are very host-specific. A bird species usually is host to more than one species of feather louse, and these are characteristic for the entire order or family. Kinship relations between these parasites thus give important information for evaluating the kinship relations of the various host groups.

Behavior   Not only is information for the structural characteristics of an animal organism fixed in its genes; its behavior is also genetically determined. These are called innate, or instinctive, behavior traits. Like morphological characteristics, the inborn patterns of behavior

Little Corellas (*C. s. sanguinea*) are difficult to detect in dense vegeation, although they generally occur in flocks. However, their ear-splitting screeching can be heard from far away.

Breeding pair of Major Mitchell's Cockatoos (C. l. leadbeateri). The female can be recognized by the red iris, as well as by the more extensive yellow band in the crest.

are subject to the laws of evolution; thus behavior can be a truly decisive factor in the diagnosis of a systematic arrangement. The simpler components of behavior often furnish important characteristics for differentiation; this especially holds true if closely related species are difficult to tell apart on the basis of physical characteristics alone. Clarification of the natural interrelations of closely related groups of species and genera that show great similarities in structure becomes possible by tracing the differences in behavior programs.

It is not always easy to determine whether similar behavior complexes are homologous, i.e., referable to the same genetic information, or that they developed convergently as adaptations to the environment. For instance, the undulating flight of many small birds is probably the result of aerodynamic requirements and does not indicate possible relationships. Thus particular behaviors are not a sufficient basis for clarification; instead, comparisons between the total behavior catalogs of different species are necessary. Social behavior (i.e., behavior patterns directed toward conspecifics) can provide especially strong evidence since behavior patterns associated with abiotic factors are often more heavily subject to evolutionary change. Ontogeny is also significant; frequently animals of closely related species behave much more similarly in the early stages of development than in the adult state. With few exceptions, parrots are social birds; i.e., they live together in groups. Social ties exist between the individual members, yet these are subordinate to the pair bond. These birds are monogamous, and mates probably will remain together for life, even within the flock; observations to the contrary in captivity can probably be traced back to behavior abnormalities or forced pairings. Larger species mature sexually between two and five years of age. As with European corvids, pair bonding often takes place much earlier, so firmly paired immature birds may be found even in a flock of youngsters. Here an animal learns about food acquisition and the

recognition and avoidance of enemies—experiences important for the survival of the species. While in some parrot species individuals remain together in flocks even during the breeding season (e.g., members of the genus *Agapornis*), in most the onset of the urge to reproduce counteracts the flock instinct. This must be viewed in the context of the survival of the species; the availability of both suitable nesting cavities and food for rearing the brood are the decisive factors here.

It has already been mentioned that most parrots are cavity breeders. Males and females cooperate in rearing the young, which are given food from the crop. This example clearly demonstrates that the ancestry of a bird species cannot be decided on the basis of a single behavioral character. Rather, it is necessary to examine its entire behavioral repertoire. Once it has become clear which feeding technique this or that parrot species employs to rear its young, only then can this behavior be used as a taxonomic component in the systematization of families and species.

How to Recognize a Cockatoo   The most striking external character of all cockatoos is the movable crest, which is more or less pronounced, depending on genus and species. In the sole member of the genus *Probosciger*, the Palm Cockatoo, it consists of long, backward-curving feathers, wide at the base and tapering to a point. On the other hand, the black cockatoos, which are grouped in the genus *Calyptorhynchus*, have a short, close-fitting crest. The monotypic genus *Callocephalon*—its only member is the Gang-gang Cockatoo—is recognizable by its forward-curving crest of plumulaceous feathers. The Galah, placed in the genus *Eolophus*, has a short crest that lies flat. The so-called white cockatoos grouped in the genus *Cacatua* exhibit the most diverse crest shapes; this led Mathews to separate them into various subgroups. The crests of the Sulphur-crested (*C. galerita*), Lesser Sulphur-crested (*C. sulphurea*), and Major Mitchell's (*C.

leadbeateri) cockatoos consist of wide, rather long, forward-pointing feathers. The Blue-eyed *(C. ophthalmica)* and Salmon-crested *(C. moluccensis)* cockatoos represent transitions to the White Cockatoo *(C. alba)*. As in the former, the head adornment of the White Cockatoo curves back, but the feathers atop the head are very broad and comparatively long. The Red-vented *(C. haematuropygia)*, Little Corella *(C. sanguinea)*, Goffin's *(C. goffini)*, Long-billed *(C. tenuirostris)*, and Ducorps's *(C. ducorpsii)* cockatoos—all often called round-crested—have short, broad-feathered, mostly close-fitting crests. Finally, the Cockatiel is distinguished by a fine, narrow, tapered crest that can be raised or lowered according to the degree of excitement. This is also true for all other species of cockatoos; the crest has trigger functions in the behavior of the animals. A member of the family Psittacidae, the Horned Parakeet *(Eunymphicus cornutus)* also has a feather crest, but unlike those of cockatoos, it consists of only two elongated feathers.

Another immediately evident morphological characteristic of many cockatoo species is the ear patches which are a different color from the body plumage. Characteristic of the Cockatiel *(N. hollandicus)*, the Yellow-tailed *(C. f. funereus)* and White-tailed *(C. f. baudinii)* Black, and the Lesser Sulphur-crested *(C. sulphurea)* cockatoos, this is hinted at in other species at least in the plumage of the young. In location, they are clearly different from the well-defined cheek spots of the rosellas *(Platycercus* spp.).

The structure and form of the tail feathers differ from species to species. The cockatoos have short tails, compared to their body length. The individual feathers are not gradated relative to one another. Only the outermost feathers are somewhat shorter, which gives the tail its rounded shape. The Cockatiel *(N. hollandicus)*, on the other hand, has a comparatively long tail. The tail feathers are gradated in such a way that they increase in length from the outside in toward the center; however, this is not as regular as with the rosellas. The two central tail feathers diverge completely from the pattern; they are about 2 cm. longer than the two adjacent feathers.

Great distances must be traversed flying in search of food; the pointed shape of the Cockatiel's wings makes it an elegant flying acrobat. As a rule, all cockatoos are good, skillful fliers; usually not particularly fast, they instead have good endurance. The structure of the primaries is the same in cockatoos as in rosellas. In all species, the second through fifth primaries are strongly indented.

Although the coloration of the plumage varies greatly among the species—the palette ranges from black through brown, gray, and pink to white—some important correspondences may be noted. The plumage colors result from actual colors (melanins and carotenoids), and the structural color white is also very common. On the other hand, neither structural blue nor the mixed colors green and violet are found in cockatoos.

The shape and size of the beak are species-characteristic. In this connection the diverse feeding habits of the animals must be considered. These have been investigated most thoroughly in the black cockatoos, resulting in the division of the genus *Calyptorhynchus* into two groups by various authors. The Black Cockatoo *(C. funereus)* has a comparatively narrow beak, in which the upper mandible is elongated and pointed; this enables it to dig in rotting wood in order to reach insect larvae. On the other hand, the Red-tailed Cockatoo *(C. magnificus)* has a broad, blunt beak which is less suited for digging but ideal for cracking seeds and nuts. The Glossy Cockatoo *(C. lathami)* is recognizable by its wide, protruding beak (among other things), with which it can easily take apart the *Casuarina* cones which are its preferred food. In the genus *Cacatua,* the Long-billed Corella *(C. tenuirostris)* offers the clearest example of the interrelation between bill structure and way of life: with their long, tapered, pointed upper mandibles, the birds are especially well suited for digging up roots and sprouting seeds from the ground.

Galah (*E. r. roseicapillua*), male.

Above: A pair of Galahs (*E. r. assimilis*)
engaged in social grooming. Photographed in
central Australia near Alice Springs.
Right: Galah (*E. r. roseicapillus*) at the nesting
cavity, near Mildura, Victoria. This pair
removed the bark from the lower part of the
trunk to make the approach of intruders more
difficult.

In the Cockatiel (*N. hollandicus*), the Palm (*P. aterrimus*) and Gang-gang (*C. fimbriatum*) cockatoos, and the Galah (*E. roseicapillus*), as well as in some members of the genus *Cacatua*, the cere is feathered; however, all of the black cockatoos have a naked cere.

An anatomical characteristic common to all cockatoos is found in their skull structure; the lacrimal and temporal bones in cockatoos are joined by a narrow band of bone so that the eye socket is closed like a ring.

The examples listed demonstrate clearly the relation between body structure of an animal and its environment; among other things, the basis for the evolution of differing species can be found here. The availability of new ecological niches to the operation of selective advantage is one reason why, despite a lack of geographical isolation, new races or species, which no longer mix with one another, may emerge. The significance of ecological niches for the formation of races and species was already demonstrated by Charles Darwin in the case of the Galapagos finches.

The great uniformity within the order of parrots of all the characteristics listed makes possible, on one hand, the clear separation of this group from the other orders; on the other hand, convincing relationships between this order and other groups can scarcely be proven. Today, parrots are placed close to the pigeons. Because of this great uniformity, the systematic subdivision of the order of parrots presents further difficulties; the ranking of the various groups has not been sufficiently clarified to this day. Almost as great as the number of scientific publications about parrots is the number of different classifications proposed. In comparing the writings of different authors—the names Gould (1865), Thompson (1900), Reichenow (1913), Neunzig (1921), Peters (1937), Berndt and Meise (1962), Brereton (1962, 1963), Immelmann (1962, 1971), Boetticher (1964), Forshaw (1969, 1971, 1981), Smith (1975), and Wolters (1975) have been consulted here—one meets with ever-diverging systematic arrangements.

The following summary shows Forshaw's arrangement (1971). In *Parrots of the World*, he divides the order Psittaciformes into three families, which he further divides into subfamilies. (The genera which compose the family of cockatoos are also given here.)

Order **Psittaciformes** (parrots)
  Family **Loriidae** (lories)
  Family **Cacatuidae** (cockatoos)
    Subfamily **Cacatuinae**
      Genus *Probosciger* (Palm Cockatoo)
      Genus *Calyptorhynchus* (black cockatoos)
      Genus *Callocephalon* (Gang-gang Cockatoo)
      Genus *Eolophus* (Galah)
      Genus *Cacatua* (white cockatoos)
    Subfamily **Nymphicinae**
      Genus *Nymphicus* (Cockatiel)
  Family **Psittacidae**
    Subfamily **Nestorinae**
    Subfamily **Micropsittinae**
    Subfamily **Psittacinae**
    Subfamily **Strigopinae**

In the second edition of *Australian Parrots*, Forshaw (1981) follows extensively the classification proposed by Smith: the cockatoos constitute one of three subfamilies within the single family Psittacidae. He separates the tribe Cacatuini from the tribe Calopsittacini, which contains the single genus *Nymphicus* (Cockatiel).

These two examples show the problems involved in the systematization of this order. It is established that the cockatoos constitute a closely related group within the parrots; whether they should have the rank of family or subfamily will not be decided here. In the following pages the earlier arrangement of Forshaw (1971) will be adhered to, especially since it does not differ from the more recent treatment in as far as sequence is concerned. A less controversial question is the subdivision into various genera; throughout what follows, the genera set out by Forshaw are employed. The treatment of the various species and subspecies is also problematical; for this, see the sections dealing with the species.

Cockatoo Behavior

Field Observations With a few exceptions, parrots are social birds. This signifies animals living companionably together in lasting pairs, families, or groups. Usually this is an advantage to the individual animal. The size of the flock varies not only from species to species, but must also be viewed in the context of its habitat. Thus species which inhabit tropical forest regions can be observed mostly in smaller groups which often are casual assemblages, but in part also amount to family units. Inaccessible habitats and the dense leafy canopy of the forest render the opportunities for observation difficult, so few observations of these species in the wild have been made. Conversely, the inhabitants of the dry regions of Australia's interior often unite in large flocks and exhibit, by way of adaptation to the irregular precipitation, a nomadic lifestyle. Here, the frequency of occurrence of the various species is determined by the food supply. Customarily, cockatoos may be observed eating on the ground in pairs or small flocks; to this are added sexually immature birds, because the protection offered and the social relationships within the flock are especially significant for young birds. Here pair bonding begins, as mates find each other not only when they have reached sexual maturity. Larger flocks assemble especially during migrations. During periods of drought, certain areas in which a species of cockatoo used to be numerous are abandoned. Thus, in the Australian interior, Little Corellas *(C. sanguinea)* or Galahs *(E. roseicapillus)* may form flocks which consist of more than a thousand individuals. It is easy to imagine the enormous damage such a flock can cause in a grain field.

Being nomadic species, many cockatoos are good colonizers, because with their appearance (sedentary birds usually occur singly in strange regions) the growth of new populations in areas hitherto unvisited becomes possible. If natural barriers are lacking in their range, a constant intermixing of genetic material takes place; this explains the fact that there are no subspecies of the Cockatiel *(N. hollandicus).* Conversely, new species or subspecies or both were able to develop by evolution in the course of millennia in isolated regions. This is true in the extreme for island populations; the six subspecies of the Lesser Sulphur-crested Cockatoo *(C. sulphurea)* are a pertinent example.

The nomadic way of life and the formation of flocks entail changes in behavior. Group behavior dominates over individual behavior to safeguard the integrity of the flock. Through a transfer of mood, all the animals follow roughly the same daily rhythm; they rest, eat, and groom together. In the course of phyletic history, flock-maintaining signals developed, which may be visual as well as aural. For example, the white wing markings of the Cockatiel *(N. hollandicus)* or the pink under wing coverts of the Galah *(E. roseicapillus)* must be interpreted as a signal directed at the flock, whether in a male, female, or juvenile. In addition, in almost all species of cockatoos a contact call can be heard.

Together with group behavior, certain mechanisms that are of advantage to the individual animal within the group were developed. One of these is the alarm system widespread among cockatoos. When the parrots leave their sleeping places after morning grooming (usually the same sites are occupied every evening), never will all flock members land in the same place for feeding. There will always be several animals that will seek out elevated spots from which they can survey the surroundings. If an emergency arises, these sentinels

Above: Red-tailed Cockatoos (*C. m.magnificus*) in flight. The sexes can be distinguished readily by the differently colored tail bands. This marking has a signalling function not only in courtship; in flight it ensures that the flock keep together.
Left: Palm Cockatoo (*P. a. goliath*) threatening the observer.

Above: Sulphur-crested Cockatoos (*C. g. galerita*). This picture was taken in early spring in the mountains of the Great Dividing Range, near the national capital, Canberra. Right: After being disturbed at the nest box, the male Little Corella (*C. s. sanguinea*) threatens the supposed enemy.

alert their fellows by shrill cries which effect the hasty departure of the flock. This behavior can be observed in the Red-tailed Cockatoo (*C. magnificus*), for instance. It is found mostly in small flocks of fifteen to twenty animals, and during feeding one or two will always remain off to the side of an elevated post in order to warn other flock members in case of danger. Sulphur-crested Cockatoos (*C. galerita*) exhibit the same behavior, and Galahs (*E. roseicapillus*) like to associate with them; Galahs themselves have no sentinel system, so they profit by the warnings of the Sulphur-crested Cockatoos. Little Corellas (*C. sanguinea*), inhabitants of the steppes, have developed a special warning system. They spend the greater part of the day on the ground, where they eat all kinds of seeds. Even during the breeding season they fly in flocks as they search for food, and their courtship also takes place essentially on the ground. Living in the steppes, they are not in a position to post lookouts up high, so there are always several animals—the number depends on the size of the flock—that will fly up for a short time. They will rise only a few meters above the ground and immediately land again in the same spot. If danger is sighted, they utter alarm calls, and the entire flock flees.

In captivity as in the wild, there is necessarily an increase in social confrontations as the group or flock grows. A peck order is unthinkable in larger gatherings because, for one thing, the animals would exhaust themselves in fights for rank; for another, this presupposes that the animals know each other individually. The size of the flock precludes both. In a flock the space available to each individual is small, hence the acquisition and maintenance of a territory is impossible. The resulting increase in aggression must be allayed by the group members; otherwise, flock integrity would not be possible. In the course of phylogeny, mechanisms to counter the disposition to aggression had to be developed to permit the proximity of individuals. Thus aggression and individual distance are small in those cockatoos that form flocks outside the breeding season. *Individual distance* describes the proximity to others of the same species without aggressive action resulting. It is dependent on the individual's mood and the activity entailed, as well as on the size of the group. When a flock of cockatoos invades a grain field, the animals will usually feed in immediate proximity to one another, without any confrontations occurring.

Both flock size and individual distance vary according to the motivation of the animals. Therefore, during the breeding season the behavior of most cockatoo species changes. The impetus to breed opposes the flock instinct, and an enlargement of individual space results. If certain limits are transgressed, aggressive actions will follow; therefore, in the course of phyletic history inhibiting mechanisms between mates and within the family had to be developed. This change in behavior during the reproductive season serves to perpetuate the species. Dispersion throughout the whole breeding area guarantees a food supply sufficient for the brood; the search for a nesting site is also facilitated.

Cockatoos breed in cavities in trees or branches, preferring dead trees from which they can survey the area. In rotting tree trunks, the animals dig their own cavities or enlarge preexisting ones. In most instances, the eggs are deposited on the half-rotted wood remnants; the addition of nesting material is known only in the Galah (*E. roseicapillus*) and the Palm Cockatoo (*P. aterrimus*). In the former, another very interesting behavioral trait can be observed. Galahs (*E. roseicapillus*) remove the bark around the entrance to the breeding cavity and then polish the trunk to a mirror-like smoothness with their beaks, but also using the oily dust of the powder downs. On inclined branches, only the inside of the branch is polished. Though the reason for this behavior has not been explained sufficiently, it is thought to be a defense against predators. Entering the nest cavity is made more difficult for nest robbers.

Of interest are the distribution of nest sites

and the extent to which pairs tolerate others of the same species in the vicinity. Thus, with the Little Corella *(C. sanguinea)* or the Galah *(E. roseicapillus)*, several nests are often found on one breeding tree; on the other hand, the nests of Cockatiels *(N. hollandicus)* are never found grouped on one tree or nearby; usually they are more than 200 m. away from each other. Despite these exceptions, it can be stated generally that species inhabiting the savanna, because of more widely available food, exhibit behavior more markedly social than those cockatoo species inhabiting forests.

The reproductive behavior of the cockatoos appears to be determined by external factors. If certain conditions are met—namely abundance of food, sufficient temperature and light, and a nesting cavity—animals in captivity will breed all year long, with the exception of the main molting period. One explanation for this behavior may be found in the fact that the cockatoos in the wild are not dependent on a fixed breeding season either. The breeding season of the Cockatiel *(N. hollandicus),* for instance, depends exclusively on climatic factors, especially rain. Customarily the animals breed between August and December, but nests may also be found in April. Because of the size of its range and the concomitant variations in climate and food availability, the Galah *(E. roseicapillus)* must also adjust its behavior to external factors. As an inhabitant of the dry regions of central Australia, it must breed as quickly as possible once it finds favorable living conditions, in order to guarantee the survival of the species. Consequently, according to Forshaw, the Galah breeds between June and November in the north, and between August and January in the southern part of the continent.

Immelmann describes a similar situation for the Budgerigar *(Melopsittacus undulatus):* "For rearing its young, the Budgerigar depends on half-ripe seeds, which are available only after a rainfall has triggered a new vegetation cycle. Since the rainfall in central Australia is irregular, the Budgerigar is not tied to certain months of the year, but times its reproduction solely by the rains. Regularity can be found only in that the rains in the southern part of its range are more frequent in the winter semester, but are more frequent during the summer in the north. Thus in the south, clutches are found more often in the spring months of October and November, and in the north during February and March." Other species with irregular breeding seasons, according to Immelmann, are Bourke's Parakeet *(Neophema bourkii),* the Princess Parrot *(Polytelis alexandrae),* and the Night Parrot *(Geopsittacus occidentalis).* All three species are inhabitants of the arid regions of central Australia.

Conditions are different for the inhabitants of the coastal regions of the Australian continent. In the south, breeding takes place in the months from August to December. During this time, the temperatures are like central European summer temperatures, and, in addition, sufficient seed is still available because of the winter rains. During the summer the vegetation dies, and the breeding season comes to an end. A second breeding is possible in April and May if the autumn rains begin early. In northern Australia, it is warm enough all year around, so breeding seasons of the species living there are regulated by the precipitation. They breed in the months from December through April, because rainfall is regular during that period. Similar constraints apply to inhabitants of islands. Here too the breeding season depends entirely on rain and the consequent availability of food. Forshaw mentions the period April through June as breeding time for the White *(C. alba)* and Salmon-crested *(C. moluccensis)* cockatoos, but these species can be bred year around in indoor aviaries without any problems.

Maintenance Activities   The patterns of behavior grouped under this heading are of special importance to properly maintain body metabolism and can be observed daily in healthy animals.

Above: Red-tailed Cockatoos (*C. m. magnificus*). The light upper mandible and yellow spotting indicate that there are females or young birds not yet in full color here. The bird perched alone in the middle of the picture is a male.

Left: Galahs (*E. r. roseicapillus*) often exhibit identical behavior through mood transfer. In extreme instances, certain behavior elements —in this case, stretching—are completely synchronized.

Right: Galahs (*E. r. assimilis*) foraging at the side of the road.
Below: Ducorps's Cockatoos (*C. ducorpsii*) are often taken from their nests by natives and kept as tame pets.

Locomotion On the ground, all cockatoos exhibit the typical "waddling" gait. The intertarsal joints touch the ground and supply additional support with each step, while the body executes weaving motions. In the trees, on the other hand, cockatoos walk extremely dexterously; one foot is positioned in front of the other, and the body turns in the direction of the branch. Only the Cockatiel (*N. hollandicus*) departs from this pattern; it walks like the Budgerigar (*Melopsittacus undulatus*), sideways along the branch, setting one foot parallel to the other. Locomotion by hopping on both feet is typical of the pointed-crest cockatoos especially; it is hardly ever observed in round-crested cockatoos, and never in black cockatoos (*Calyptorhynchus*). Usually this mode of locomotion is chosen only during climbing and walking, when the next point fixed visually is too far away to be reached with the beak. That all cockatoos are excellent climbers must certainly be taken into consideration when caring for them in captivity. Like all parrots, they use the beak as a third leg. Climbing serves mainly for bridging short distances.

Larger distances are traversed by flight. The inhabitants of the savanna regions of central Australia particularly excel as flyers; this should be considered when planning an aviary. Galahs (*E. roseicapillus*) are capable of amazing flight maneuvers, even in a very limited space. Steppe birds especially tend to fly away in a panic if they are alarmed. As inhabitants of open terrain that can be surveyed easily by preying enemies and that offers hardly any hiding places, they hurl themselves upward at great speed and flee great distances if they are in danger. Even Cockatiels (*N. hollandicus*) bred here still show this behavioral trait; in panic they often fail to notice obstacles and wire mesh and collide with them. The instinct of an individual to flee is communicated instantly to the other members of the flock and triggers the same instinctive reaction in them. This social phenomenon is easy to observe once one knows the warning system of cockatoos. Species that inhabit forests, though they ordinarily move through their natural biotope by climbing, are also capable of skilled flight maneuvers. The author's White Cockatoo (*C. alba*) shows amazing skill in its flights around the room; it has never collided with furniture or windows or damaged any objects, as free-flying amazons (*Amazona* spp.) or Grey Parrots (*Psittacus erithacus*) often do.

Feeding According to Berndt and Meise, Cockatiels (*N. hollandicus*), unlike all other cockatoos, do not transport food to the beak with the foot; this statement must be contradicted here. Although this behavior is not so frequent as among members of the subfamily Cacatuinae, which regularly use the foot as an implement for eating, Cockatiels (*N. hollandicus*) will occasionally grip food with a foot and transport it to the beak. Therefore, the technique appears to be firmly anchored in the instinctive behavior of the animals, though Cockatiels employ it considerably less frequently than do the other cockatoos.

The drinking behavior of cockatoos is interesting and completely different from that of other parrots. While the beak is immersed in the water, the animal executes scooping movements with its beak. Next, the head is lifted and tilted back; rapid movements of the tongue and hasty swallows can be observed. Larger species sometimes lap up the water with their agile tongues, but after this the head is always tilted back, and swallowing follows. Most other parrots make no scooping movements with their lower mandibles, and the head is not tilted back afterwards. They merely immerse their mandibles in the water, lift their heads, draw up any water adhering to the beak with their tongues, and then swallow. That such behavior by itself cannot be used to determine the phyletic history of a group of birds is shown by pigeons and grouse, which drink by sucking. Many pigeons suck the water up, using their beaks like a straw; this is possible only if the nostrils can be closed by a flap. At first glance, grouse do the same, but closer observation reveals differences from the sucking of pigeons. In this case, behavior is not an indicator of relationship.

Resting and Sleeping Healthy birds rest on one leg, with the other drawn up toward the belly. The plumage is ruffled up, blinking slows down, and the eyes are partially or completely closed. Even during the day occasionally, the head is turned toward the back for sleeping and, after a few settling movements, hidden in the feathers of the back up to the base of the bill. Firmly paired animals rest and sleep close to each other; the individual distance in these instances is almost nil.

Usually the same sleeping places are sought out every evening. This should be considered when accustoming animals to new surroundings. If they are chased into the shelter room of the aviary for sleeping for the first few days, they will soon go in on their own. A perch installed as high as possible will help considerably. During the breeding season, the males sleep outside the nest box, but always nearby. The females will sleep in the box at night, even after the young have hatched—at first on top of, afterward beside, the young. The young are also being fed. Once fledged, they usually will not return to the breeding cavity to sleep.

Temperature Regulation In cold weather, the ruffled plumage forms a cushion of air that insulates the body. If it is very warm, the feathers are kept tight against the body and the wings are lifted slightly; all activity takes place in the early morning and late afternoon.

Most species of cockatoos avoid too much exposure to the sun; for this reason, the animals should be given the opportunity to sit in the shade if they desire. This is especially true for those that inhabit tropical rain forests. Kenning observed that during midday wild female Cockatiels *(N. hollandicus)* would often hang head downward in front of the nest cavity, fanning the air with their wings.

Comfort Behavior This concept covers two different groups of behaviors: the matter of grooming (preening and scratching movements), and movements related to body metabolism, particularly its oxygenation (stretching movements, yawning). However, the application of this concept is not entirely consistent.

Grooming Activities in this function cluster are common in all cockatoos and can be observed during almost all times of the day. Such preening episodes are most often initiated by ruffling the contour feathers with the beak. Cleaning the wing and tail feathers very often follows immediately. As the intensity of cleaning increases, a change to rubbing movements with beak or head in the powder-down areas can be observed: the powder is rubbed on and distributed throughout the plumage with rapid movements. The breast and belly feathers are not powdered, probably because these body areas do not become as wet in the rain. Extensive preening episodes can be observed after resting periods especially. Mood transfer is even stronger with this behavior than with others.

Stretching Most cockatoos live together in groups. In a society of this kind it is important for all the animals to engage in the same activities at the same time; only in this way is the integrity of the flock guaranteed. Hence the mood transfers which can be observed must be considered adaptations to this lifestyle. In extreme cases, it may happen that in firmly paired animals certain sequences of movements, e.g., stretching, take place almost synchronously. The movements themselves are similar for all parrots. One wing and one leg on the same side of the body are extended backwards; at the same time, the tail is fanned out and turned toward that side of the body. These stretching movements are often repeated several times and are frequently correlated with yawning. Each stretch is almost always followed by a second movement in which both wings are lifted, either folded or only slightly spread.

Left: Mutual preening in Little Corellas (*C. s. sanguinea*) to reinforce pair bonding after being threatened by an observer.
Below: Little Corellas (*C. s. sanguinea*) drinking in the shallow man-made lake at Fogg Dam near Darwin.

Above: Galahs (*E. r. assimilis*). The naked gray eye ring permits accurate subspecific identification even in this flight photo.
Right: Galah (*E. r. roseicapillus*) gnawing at the entrance of the nesting cavity.

Bathing Here one must distinguish between a rain bath and bathing in a water container. The latter—at least in captivity—is regularly seen in breeding animals toward the end of the incubation period; apparently it serves to regulate the humidity of the air in the breeding cavity. All species of cockatoos, including the Cockatiel (*N. hollandicus*), like to bathe in the rain. This behavior is initiated by extreme ruffling of the feathers and slight lifting of the wings. As the intensity increases, the wings are completely spread. Flapping the wings and turning the body are behaviors that frequently occur next. Often the animals will hang head downward on a branch or on the wire mesh in order to give the feathers a better soaking. This behavior should be taken into account when keeping cockatoos in captivity. A sprinkler installed in an outdoor aviary will serve very well. Cockatoos that are kept indoors should be offered regular showers with a plant mister.

Scratching A behavior pattern often invoked in the systematization of parrots is head scratching. Cockatiels (*N. hollandicus*), like rosellas (*Platycercus* spp.), scratch their heads from over their wings; i.e., they move their feet to their heads over the wing from behind, and scratch rapidly with the claw of the outer toe. This behavior is the opposite of that observable in the Cacatuinae. Cockatoos scratch themselves from under the wings; i.e., they bring the foot to the head in the same way as when holding food. As a rule, all cockatoos scratch themselves like this, contrary to de Grahl's statement. However, behavior that departs from the Cockatiel's normal pattern occasionally can be seen. Scratching movements like those of the cockatoos also can be observed, though not particularly often. Similarly divergent behavior has been described by Brereton and Immelmann in the Galah (*E. roseicapillus*). Some individuals will repeatedly scratch in a manner not normal for the species: over the wing from behind. The frequency of scratching was also uncharacteristically low in these cases.

These observations show clearly that both patterns of behavior exist, at least rudimentarily, in many parrots, but that one of these behavior patterns is clearly dominant over the other. The manner of scratching alone does not permit a statement about kinship; this is shown by the fact that such closely related species as the Red-winged Parrot (*Aprosmictus erythropterus*) and the Australian King Parrot (*Alisterus scapularis*) scratch their heads completely differently.

Social Behavior This concept comprises all forms of behavior which are directed toward others of the same species. The word *social* as used in behavioral science is completely free of any values; this cannot be compared to the way it is used in human society. Social behavior permits communication within the species; all forms of behavior that take place between the members of a species may be called social. In addition to courtship and brood care, aggressive confrontations therefore must also be included.

As mentioned previously, most cockatoos are social animals that live in a permanent relationship with certain others of the same species; the associated space problems of individual animals have already been mentioned. In the course of phyletic history, mechanisms to counteract the readiness for aggression had to be developed to allow individual animals to approach within a short distance. This applies especially to mates or within a family; individual distances of very narrow compass exist here as well, and must be overcome, during copulation, for instance. Thus behaviors were built into the instinctive apparatus: on one hand to diminish existing tendencies to flee, and on the other to counteract and inhibit any aggression present. Only in this way is the perpetuation of the species ensured.

Social Feather Grooming Mate scratching frequently can be observed in all cockatoos except the genus *Probosciger*. Two purposes can be ascribed to this behavior: it serves to care for plumage areas that are accessible to the animal only with difficulty or not at all, and it also has soothing and pair-bonding functions. This becomes especially evident in conflict situations. Mutual preening can always be observed when an animal leaves the nest box to be relieved during incubation; scratching and being scratched in turn last for some minutes. The one being preened shows clear signs of enjoyment; its eyes are partly or completely closed and its head is turned to present the preferred spots at the base of the beak and around the ear to the mate. Grooming, in addition to the functions of initiating and deepening the pair bond, also serves to enhance the readiness to defend the nesting territory and to lessen any tendencies to flee. Finally, to a great extent it inhibits the redirection of aggression toward the mate. This aggression-inhibiting effect becomes particularly evident if one knows that most cockatoos preen each other extensively before copulation; reduction of the individual distance to a value of zero becomes possible only in this way.

The actions of this function cluster are common in all cockatoos; the exception of Palm Cockatoo (*P. aterrimus)* has been mentioned before. However, their intensity varies from species to species: While Cockatiels (*N. hollandicus)* limit themselves to scratching in the area of the head, the black cockatoos (*Calyptorhynchus* spp.) frequently preen each others' entire plumage, especially the rump feathers. Galahs (*E. roseicapillus)*—just like Sulphur-crested (*C. galerita),* Lesser Sulphur-crested (*C. sulphurea),* and Major Mitchell's (*C. leadbeateri)* cockatoos —preen not only each other's head feathers, but also the body plumage, with the exception of the breast and abdominal areas. Occasionally, some wing and tail feathers are pulled through the beak; this may be observed frequently in the Salmon-crested (*C. moluccensis)* and the White (*C. alba)* cockatoos in particular.

While the intent to preen is normally predominant in all these movements, they become more and more a ritual in conflict situations. The concept of *ritualized behavior* describes those patterns of behavior which have undergone a change in significance in the course of evolution and now are increasingly used for mutual communication. In the Little Corella (*C. sanguinea),* preening movements can be neatly distinguished according to the two original functions previously mentioned. If they serve indeed for grooming, they are slow and careful; preening movements take place in the region of the head as well as in the rest of the body feathers. In conflict situations, however—e.g., when the animals feel threatened by an observer—a strongly ritualized preening of the head feathers can be observed. The movements become rapid and careless; arranging the feathers and the nibbling motion of the tongue now have a subordinate role only. Hasty beak movements, limited to ruffling the plumage of the mate, take their place.

Mate Feeding Mate feeding is observed in only a few species of cockatoos. Carried over from the function cluster related to care of the brood, it is incorporated into the function cluster related to courtship as an appeasing behavior element. Mate feeding can be seen only when the animals are in the mood to breed; it does not occur as neutral pair behavior in adult animals outside the breeding season. During breeding, mate feeding serves to provision the incubating female. From the behavior of other parrot species, it can be noted among them that only the females incubate. They rarely leave the nesting cavity, either to defecate or to drink. If the instinctive bonds between the mates of a pair are intact, the female feeds only rarely, but is fed in or out of the breeding cavity by the male. In addition to this, probably original significance, mate feeding has an additional, important purpose: it serves to reinforce pair bonding, and as such can be considered an element of courtship. Inherent tendencies to flee are diminished, and the close bodily contact required for copulation is facilitated. The behavior of the female probably has an appeasing function: while fed she assumes a stance

Facing page: Pair of Lesser Sulphur-crested Cockatoos (C. sulphurea).

Major Mitchell's Cockatoos (C. l. leadbeateri) on a nesting tree, near Wyperfeld National Park in Victoria. The female is scratching her head in the manner characteristic of all cockatoos.

Male Little Corella (C. s. sanguinea) feeding a fledged youngster.

similar to that of a begging young bird.

The family of cockatoos can be divided into two groups according to incubation behavior: in one, only the females incubate; in the other, both partners incubate. The representatives of the first group exhibit mate feeding before and during incubation, so this action fulfills the same functions as in other parrot species. In those cockatoo species in which males participate in incubation, mate feeding is not seen. (Those animals which are advertised with the notation "Will feed each other" appear to be ab- normal in their behavior; however, the ir- regularity is likely to be found in the business ethics of the seller.) There is no need to supply the mate with food; because they take turns in- cubating, the female has sufficient time to feed herelf. The absence of mate feeding as an ele- ment of courtship seems to prove that this behavior originates in nutritional and physiological needs. The function of mate feeding in pair bonding is assumed by social grooming, which serves the same purpose: to diminish aggression.

Agonistic Behavior This concept includes all patterns of behavior that are part of the function cluster related to fighting and fleeing. The readiness to attack and fight or to flee depends on the place of the animal within the group, particularly its position relative to its opponent, and on its mood. Fight and fleeing behaviors are easiest to observe during the breeding season. Frequently one flows into the other. The antagonism of the aggression instinct and the fleeing instinct leads to an inner conflict which is mirrored in the actions of the cockatoo. Thus in the case of only a weak aggressive tendency, all movements in the direction of the opponent are invariably followed by retreats.

The behavior with the least aggressive intent is intimidation. These actions function to give the body a particular appearance. By swaggering broadly and forcefully, by raising the crest, spreading the wings, or fanning the tail, the body is made to look larger. The crest especially, different in color from the rest of the head plumage, may be considered to particularly function as a signal. This is true in the extreme with Major Mitchell's Cockatoo (C. leadbeateri). Spreading the wings, often combined with forward bowing—and sometimes jerky, twisting motions of the body as well—is common in many species. An intimidation flight is the rule for all species; intimidation calls can often be heard.

Behavior patterns connected with threat are much more strongly motivated by aggression. These are very much affected by the situation; it can be noted generally that readiness to attack increases with a growing reproductive urge. The behavioral conflict between attacking and fleeing is always clearly indicated by the cockatoos' threat behavior. In cases of slight intensity, the bend of the wing is slightly spread, the tail fanned, and the body does rocking movements; the last may be interpreted as ritualized attack or fleeing behavior. With more intense conflict, the wings are fully extended, and the rocking body movements become stronger. The body turns, which may be seen

as pure show; on the other hand, it exposes the ambivalence of the animal: the body faces the opponent and turns away from it.

A behavior characteristic of the cockatoo is beak clapping; the upper mandible hits the lower, making clapping noises.

Reproductive Behavior The mostly external control of reproductive behavior has been mentioned previously. If cockatoos are kept indoors, courtship, breeding, and rearing young are possible at any time of the year.

Courtship behavior is a phylogenetic pattern, an amalgam formed by the conflict of various motivations. Between the individuals of a species, attracting and repelling forces are in play, and the latter must be overcome. Conspecifics emit aggression-releasing signals, which set up a barrier to the approach of a mate; this has to be overcome if pairing is to be successful. Two appeasing elements, mate feeding and social grooming, have already been described. The behavioral conflict between pairing readiness and attack-or-flight is clearly noticeable in the courtship behavior of all cockatoos. Especially when two animals previously unknown to each other are involved, complicated courtship mechanisms precede pairing. This is evident in the comparatively simple courtship of the Cockatiel (N. hollandicus). It is characterized mostly by aggression-motivated actions derived from the function cluster related to intimidation. Only the males court actively.

Forward bows, most often coupled with intimidation strutting, are typical behaviors for most cockatoos. In those species in which the crest differs in color from the rest of the plumage, it has an important releaser function, which indicates readiness to pair. Brief preening movements in the bird's own plumage or more-or-less ritualized episodes of social grooming are often interspersed during courtship.

It is worth remarking that courtship calls become softer with the approach of laying and inception of incubation. The explanation is

44

simple: in the wild, this prevents attracting the attention of the cockatoos' enemies to the breeding cavity. The cockatoos' extremely pronounced need for gnawing becomes even more evident at the start of the reproductive period. It reaches its maximum shortly before the first egg is laid.

In cockatoos which have bred together repeatedly, copulation often takes place without courtship preceding. It can often be observed several weeks before laying, and becomes more regular in time. The readiness to mate increases, and as many as five or six copulations a day are no rarity shortly before laying. At the same time, courtship activities decrease. In cockatoos, it is usually the female that initiates copulation; her behavior stimulates the male to tread. She determines the time of copulation by assuming the typical copulatory position; absolutely still, remaining in a crouched position, with the exception of fluttering wing movements, she indicates her readiness to mate. During copulation, the female makes soft sounds, which may serve to appease possible rising aggression in the male.

Differences in incubation behavior within the family of cockatoos have been mentioned previously. Relief during incubation takes place in the manner described by K. Lorenz for doves and herons. Because of the instinctive rapport between mates, the mere appearance of one outside the breeding cavity often acts as a trigger to cause the other to leave the nest. Normal incubation relief is very simple: the incoming partner sits in the nest with the incubating one and slowly pushes it off the eggs. An actual relief ceremony is not seen; however, the appearance at the nest is announced to the incubating partner with soft beak clapping. When breeding in captivity, both adults often remain together on the clutch for prolonged periods of time, since there is no time-consuming search for food. As a rule, the females incubate at night, the males from early morning to late afternoon; several changes during the day are typical of aviary brooding.

If both adults are brooding, the young upon hatching are fed by both from the beginning. In the Palm Cockatoo *(P. aterrimus)* and the black cockatoos *(Calyptorhynchus* spp.) on the other hand, only the female feeds at first, and she is provisioned with food by the male. In this way, they avoid leaving the nest unattended; otherwise, the danger of the young falling victim to predators or of becoming chilled would be too great.

In feeding, the cockatoo parents enclose the beak of the young bird with their own, pulling the head and neck of the young up slightly and executing rapid shaking movements. The head and neck of the young bird move rhythmically up and down, while they utter peeping sounds in the same rhythm. At the same time, they spread their wings; wing trembling may be observed in all species of cockatoos during their first days of life. Feeding noises and wing trembling are important behaviors in the young; as releasing stimuli they guarantee that rearing will proceed smoothly. Weak youngsters that no longer exhibit this behavior are not fed; for the same reason, young parrots of other species are usually not accepted by cockatoo parents. Even after the young fledge, this feeding technique persists; the releaser described ensures that rearing will progress without a hitch.

Major Mitchell's Cockatoo (*C. leadbeateri*).

Male Red-tailed Cockatoo (*C. m. magnificus*) bathing in the rain, flapping his wings furiously and ruffling his body plumage.

The male Red-tail beginning his courtship display.

As courtship intensity increases, the animal fans his tail more widely, so that the red tail band becomes even more visible.

By spreading his wings wide, further apparent enlargement of the body is achieved.

Purchase and Acclimation

In captivity the cockatoo is spared important tasks, thanks to its keeper, which are essential in the wild. The daily search for food is bypassed, as is the constant need to be on the lookout for enemies; this means that a well-cared-for bird usually lives longer than it would in the wild. At the same time, captivity always means living in unnatural circumstances. Adapted optimally to all the conditions of the environment by an evolution lasting thousands of years, the animals are suddenly removed to spend the rest of their lives—for the enjoyment of their keepers—in artificially limited surroundings, e.g., with respect to climatic, nutritional, and physiological conditions. The responsibility a bird keeper takes upon himself with the purchase of an animal becomes evident.

Before purchasing a cockatoo, the first consideration should always be: Can I give my future charge at least an approximate substitute for its former life in the wild? Every bird fancier must make this decision for himself; but certain guidelines must be given here. A cockatoo is not the finishing touch of an interior decorator to fill an empty corner in an apartment. As stated repeatedly, cockatoos have a strongly developed need for social interaction; put simply, this means that the cockatoo is a gregarious bird and not a solitary bird. Its great need for social grooming illustrates this. Plainly said, this means that a cockatoo should not be a bit of nature within the four walls of a couple's home.

The need for social contact may be of great use to the keeper as far as tameness is concerned. Lacking a suitable mate, the animal becomes very close to the human; a characteristic behavior here is the presentation of ruffled neck feathers as an invitation to social grooming —therefore apparently an ideal pet bird, after all? This must be rejected, at least as far as keeping a single bird is concerned. Tame cockatoos especially may become decidedly disagreeable fellows if left alone. Bored in their small cages, they often use their already loud voices so excessively that it becomes too much for even the most patient person. The purpose of such actions is always to attract the attention of the keeper; once successful in this way, the animal, following the principle of instrumental conditioning, learns very quickly which behavior is rewarded by social contact. This author knew a Lesser Sulphur-crested Cockatoo (*C. s. citrinocristata*) which, while kept in its cage, permitted no conversation of any kind in the room. Attracting attention by constant shrieking, it rewarded attention by often bloody attacks on the hand of the keeper; after this it invited him, as usual, to scratch its head feathers. On the other hand, a neglected cockatoo may easily fall into a lethargy that sooner or later leads to impaired health.

Even if a singly kept cockatoo shows none of the behavioral disturbances mentioned, its need for contact still may not have been met adequately. Only few bird keepers have at their disposal sufficient time for the care of these birds. Since the human is only a substitute anyway, except for those birds that have been imprinted on humans since earliest youth, keeping them in pairs must always be preferred. A White Cockatoo (*C. alba*) initially kept singly by the author was an exceedingly tame and affectionate roommate and had an altogether agreeable temperament. However, it immediately formed a close attachment when offered the company of a mate, and within a few days it completely lost its customary familiarity with its keeper. Still, anyone who has ever witnessed the harmonious course of a cockatoo "marriage" will gladly put up with this disadvantage.

It goes without saying that the differing degrees of intelligence of the various species must be considered here: keeping a Salmon-crested Cockatoo *(C. moluccensis)* singly, for instance, will sooner or later bring about more problems than keeping a single Cockatiel *(N. hollandicus)*. Keeping specimens of the latter species singly may be justified, at least nowadays, since the Cockatiel is considered completely domesticated, and the demand can be met entirely by domestic breeding. Conversely, single-keeping appears all the more questionable with a species of cockatoo that has

Standard cage (measuring 45 x 45 x 75 cm.), available in either brass or chrome plating. This model is too small for permanent housing; furthermore, it will not stand up to the beaks of larger species.

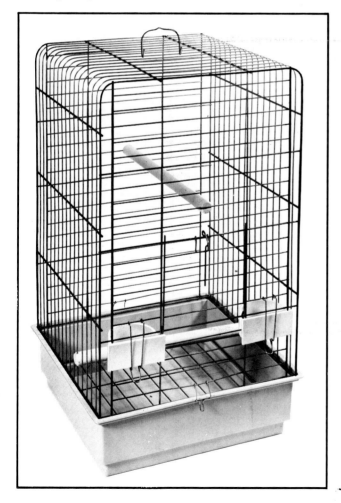

become rare in its home range—especially some island forms that have been extensively decimated by mass imports and for which no regenerating hinterland exists.

Once all these factors have been considered and the decision to purchase has been made, many things still merit attention. The purchase of live animals is a matter of trust; for this reason, the bird should be purchased from a dealer who specializes, if possible. Selection should then be made according to the maxim, Trust is good, caution is better. The quality of an animal is often very difficult even for a specialist to judge, because hidden flaws are often recognized only much later. Also, very often animals qualitatively less valuable are offered and sold. This is the reason why often all animals are advertised as young, easily tamed, talented talkers. One should never rely on such sales talk, but should make one's own choice or ask a known "nonlayman" for advice. The purchase of a bird takes time, though an attentive observer often may identify most flaws quite readily.

Particular attention must be paid to whether an animal is obviously alert and gives an impression of health, with smooth plumage, and is not hiding its head in its ruffled back feathers. In a situation with a strange observer, even a bird which is interrupted in its sleep will watch him carefully and then flee, if that is called for. If this is not the case—and if the bird, in addition, sleeps on both legs, if the plumage around the vent is dirty and sticky, if the eyes are dull and half closed—the purchase should not be made. If a cockatoo is bought from an aviary, it is more difficult to judge the state of its health, since at a distance it is hard to tell whether an animal is asleep or in ill health. It is a favorite trick of many "bird lovers" to disturb a sick animal by loud noises when approaching, so that the animal, frightened and ready to flee, is sitting sleek and ready to take off. Observation from a distance—this is also true when purchasing from a cage—can be important in such cases. The best time to purchase a bird is in the early morning hours or in the late afternoon, because the animals can be observed during their natural periods of activity.

Once an animal has been selected, it should be taken into one's hand, or the seller should be asked to hold the animal, in such a way that its nutritional state may be determined by feeling its breast muscles. The plumage also deserves particular attention at this time, since cockatoos have a tendency—the reason for this has not yet been determined—to lose wing and tail feathers, and also contour feathers, without forming new, healthy feathers. Instead, stunted and malformed feathers grow in, which are easily recognized by their abnormal shape and black quills. Malformations of the mandibles often accompany this condition. Feet and eyes also should be checked carefully; if the eyes are inflamed, no purchase should be made. Visible flaws, e.g., one-sided blindness or misshapen feet or claws, are criteria of quality in breeding birds only. Even a cockatoo with a damaged foot may become a very lovable companion if it comes into human hands when a very young bird. Here esthetic considerations should remain in the background, because such damage is often the result of capture and transport; in the wild such birds usually quickly fall prey to their enemies. As purchasers we share some of the responsibility for such damages, so we certainly should decide in favor of caring for such a bird. In agreeing on a price, allowances must be made for such things.

Another important question involves determining the age of the animal. If the bird is wanted for breeding, preference should be given to an older animal; young animals are better suited to be tame household pets. The age of a cockatoo can hardly be determined by a layman, and only with difficulty by a specialist. Males and females of the species most frequently traded may be differentiated by eye color. Females have a red iris, while the eyes of the males are entirely black. Young birds of both sexes have black eyes; the color change in females begins between one and two years and is usually completed only at four years

of age. If a cockatoo has a bright red iris, it is not a young bird. Other criteria for age determination are the eye ring in the Galah (*E. roseicapillus*)—less defined and more smooth in young birds, but more carunculate in adult animals—and the scales on the feet. The horny scales on the feet become sturdier with increasing age and have then a mostly white color; younger animals are recognizable by their darker, smoother feet. Even for breeding one should not buy birds that are too old; patience often pays off, since young birds are easier to pair.

Once purchased, it is advisable to get the animal to its destination as quickly as possible, housed in a transport box. Cages are less suitable for transport, since the excited animals tend to panic, which may lead to injuries. Before leaving for home with the precious cargo, question the seller about what the bird has been fed so far; it should continue to be fed the same, at least during the first days of acclimation. It should also be mentioned that the purchase of a bird, even without any written document, is a legal sales contract. Should there be any complaints later because of hidden faults, it is an advantage to have a witness to the transaction.

Since parrots may transmit diseases, their importation into Europe is subject to legal regulations. Ordinarily parrots imported to Germany undergo a quarantine lasting forty-five days, during which they are treated with antibiotics. The worth of these measures is controversial, because they often lead to serious damage to the internal organs, which sooner or later results in the death of the parrot. The immediate examination of fresh imports followed by specific treatment during quarantine would seem more to the point. On the other hand, an unscrupulous dealer can by-pass the regulations, set aside some of the animals, and sell them without quarantine. Although this is not usual, it happens occasionally.

The reasons listed make it clear that a newly purchased parrot, even though it outwardly appears healthy, must never be put in with

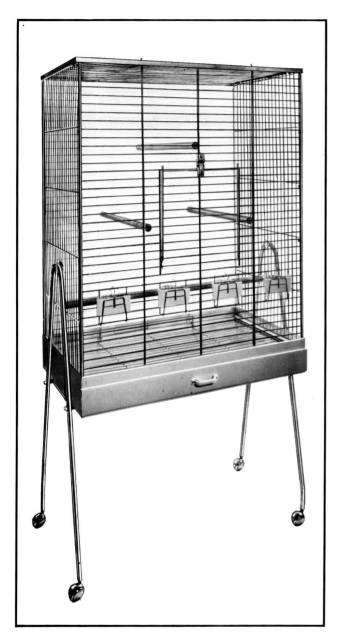

Large cage (measuring 80 x 50 x 106 cm.) which can be used as a breeding cage for small species of cockatoos, if necessary.

previously owned stock. This is also true for a bird bought from a breeder, even if the previous owner has given the impression of being very orderly and conscientious. Parrots may be permanent reservoirs of diseases without showing any of the clinical signs themselves. New acquisitions must therefore be kept isolated. A fecal specimen sent to an animal-health laboratory will provide a quick assessment of the bird's state of health. In the interest of the bird, one should always assume that it may be ill and proceed accordingly. Extreme cleanliness is advisable. The cages should be cleaned more frequently than usual; newspaper put in the cage tray is easily changed several times daily.

The bird should be fed what it is used to; at the same time, a wider variety of food should be offered to give the animal a choice. Cockatoos are particularly stubborn. If they cannot get their customary food, they would rather starve than eat anything else as a substitute. Accustoming them to a new diet must, therefore, be done very sensitively; special attention must be given to a sufficient supply of vitamins.

The accommodations of the animal must approximate the way it was kept previously. Quarantined birds are frequently kept by the importer in very high temperatures, in order to reduce the energy expenditure needed to maintain the body temperature of the animals already weakened by transport. A conscientious dealer will slowly reduce the temperature toward the end of the quarantine period, in order to facilitate the birds' transfer to room temperatures or even to outdoor aviaries. One should inquire about this thoroughly when purchasing and take the appropriate measures oneself, if necessary.

Accommodations

By the concept of accommodations, we understand the manner of housing a bird. It is the goal of perfect accommodations to provide optimal living conditions for one's charge, as close as possible to its natural environment; of course, this can never be completely achieved. But at least some conditions must be fulfilled to allow the bird to develop properly, remain healthy, and, if possible, breed. If these are not met, sooner or later there will be some physical or psychological disturbances, which an expert observer can easily tell from the behavior of the animals. Only someone who knows and understands the behavior of his cockatoos can ensure that they stay well.

Cages Considering all the things mentioned so far, the attentive reader will see immediately that the mass-produced cage is too small a space for a cockatoo pair, and this is also true for keeping a single bird. If cage-keeping is nevertheless discussed here, it is done first for the sake of completeness and, second, to give some hints to those who currently own cockatoos. Cockatoos are by nature very lively animals that prefer to climb or fly, depending on their natural habitat. Neither mode of behavior can be fully accommodated by cage keeping—these are the overriding problems in keeping birds.

The most important principle is that a cage is often too small, but never too large. Any suggestion of measurements in these pages is purposely omitted; the only advice is "as large as possible." It need not be pointed out that the size of the cage must have a direct relation to the size of its inhabitant; the bird must have at least sufficient freedom of movement to preen its feathers and extend its wings. Even with a large cage it is necessary to allow the bird daily excursions out into the room. However, this should take place only under supervision, as will be confirmed by everyone who knows the destructive force of a cockatoo's beak. A pair of Salmon-crested Cockatoos known to the author managed, one unsupervised evening, to gnaw holes the size of soup plates into a door left ajar. Compared to Grey Parrots (*Psittacus erithacus*) and amazons (*Amazona* spp.), cockatoos are exemplary flyers, able to execute skillful turns and landings even in small rooms, causing comparatively little mischief this way. While trimming the wings inhibits the urge to move about, it also affects the bird's skill if it does attempt to fly. The danger of escape is reduced as well, and the advantage of taking the bird outdoors, at least in summer, should not be overlooked.

When purchasing and furnishing a cage, some important things must be considered. Although many styles and models are advertised for sale, most of them are unsuitable for keeping large parrots. As far as size is concerned, usually only those cages that are marketed as "room aviaries" are suitable. A cage must never be selected according to fashionable and decorative criteria. Its most essential function is not as an ornament for the home, but as the place where our charge will have to spend at least a major part of the day; however, the latter need not exclude the former. Ornamental cages are frequently much more expensive than ordinary models and are, in addition, mostly unsuitable for the birds. Round cages offer the cockatoo little opportunity for climbing, since its beak and feet find a hold only with difficulty on the mostly vertical wires; moreover, they make the practical placement of perches and climbing

Sturdy, roomy cage (measuring 68 x 70 x 100 cm.) which offers sufficient space for the larger species to move around. Horizontal wiring would be preferable.

bars more difficult. For this reason, the cage should have wires running horizontally, which enables the bird to climb without problems; wire mesh, of course, serves the same purpose.

Particular attention must be given to the material and the workmanship. A wooden framework is out of the question, not only for hygienic reasons—any mites present will find a good hiding place—but even the beak of a Lesser Sulphur-crested Cockatoo *(C. sulphurea)* is strong enough to turn such a model into kindling sooner or later. The strength of the beak with which the cockatoo will eventually attack the cage increases in proportion to body size. Thus, a White Cockatoo *(C. alba)* belonging to the author effortlessly succeeded in cracking the welds of a model advertised for large parrots; Palm Cockatoos *(P. aterrimus)* can bend even wavy wire mesh. The reasons mentioned also make it clear that adequate security for the cage door is essential; the latches installed by the manufacturer are usually opened without difficulty.

Nowadays, without exception, modern cages have a pan that is made either of hard plastic or sheet metal and a tray. In the latter, the bottom third of the cage is usually enclosed by glass on all sides in order to prevent dirtying the surroundings. Cage pans cast in one piece have the advantage of hygienic cleaning but are impractical beyond a given size because the cage wire has to be set onto the pan from above. On the other hand, cage pans with trays have the disadvantage that the edges of the tray are easily bent. A seed guard of glass panes has to be cleaned often; in addition, the sand which is used on the floor of the cage often falls out between panes and cage. If the panes are not sufficiently secure, the birds will get them out easily.

A bottom grille, which is often part of commercial cage furnishings, is not recommended, since the droppings will stick to its wires anyway, thus negating its purpose. A layer of newspaper is often said to be hygienic because it is easily changed, but a layer of bird or river sand is, in the long run, the best and also the most natural solution. Cockatoos also like to eat the grains of fresh sand. They contain some minerals which are organically important and also assist the grinding action of the ventriculus.

Commercial cages are furnished with turned hardwood perches that have the advantage of effortless cleanability; in addition, they can stand up to the cockatoo's beak, at least for a while. On the other hand, it is a disadvantage for the bird's grip to always be the same size; over a long period of time, this may result in damage to the feet. Tree branches of varying circumference are much better cage furnishings, especially since the cockatoos like to peel them. Thus, they at once satisfy the animals' urge to keep busy and supply some important elements that are contained in the tree bark. The branches should be fastened so that the bird has sufficient opportunity for climbing but its freedom of movement is not limited too much. Care must be taken to keep the lower levels and the food and water dishes free of droppings. It will frequently be necessary to install fresh branches. However, a hardwood perch should not be passed up. If it is covered with glue on the underside and then rolled in bird sand, it is, after drying, an ideal natural nail file. The claws will be worn down continually, and the distasteful capture and restraint of the birds becomes unnecessary.

Special attention must be given to the food dishes, often insufficient in number in commercial cages and often inadequately secure. Fastened by thin metal strips or wires, they are easily unhooked by the bird and land on the floor of the room, to the joy of the housewife. Not counting the drinking container, there must be at least two, or better three, dishes for each bird, which should be mounted in such a way that they are easy for the keeper to remove, impossible for the birds. We should choose materials that on one hand can withstand the parrot's beak and on the other are easy to clean. Glazed earthenware dishes have proved successful. They are mounted on a wire bridge, which is easily shaped from square wire

mesh and placed halfway up the cage. If the cage is sufficiently large, it can also be set on the floor.

Lately more and more vitrine cages are offered, and are welcomed by buyers. They usually blend visually with the room and also guarantee against dirtying the surroundings. Keeping parrots in this fashion can be recommended only within limits, since such glass cages do not provide for the climbing needs of the birds. If such a cage is sufficiently large, however, this can be partly remedied by optimal furnishings. Climbing branches skillfully fastened to the side walls will mostly accommodate the natural behavior of the animals. Care must be taken that the glass panes and branches are easily removable and replaceable for cleaning purposes. Vitrines which meet these requirements are not available commercially and must be specially built or adapted. Care must be taken to use easily cleanable materials that will also resist cockatoo beaks. Adequate ventilation and lighting must be provided.

The last topic to be considered is the location of the cage. Not just any convenient spot in the home is suitable. Most cockatoos do not appreciate direct sunlight; nevertheless, only a bright spot is suitable. Other important considerations are the following: dry-air heating impedes regrowth of the feathers; drafts may result in colds; busy locations meet the needs of the animals for social contact but always have negative consequences for breeding. These points show that no patent advice can be given, especially since it is impossible to consider all the various situations; an appeal to the sensitivity of the bird keeper must be made here.

Stands, Bow Perches, Climbing Trees Stands, bow perches, and climbing trees have limited applications in keeping cockatoos, since only tame animals can be kept this way. The meaning of *tame* is expanded here to include all birds that will not hastily take flight at the keeper's first approach, though it must be left to the keeper's sensitivity to

Stand with a sturdy tray of sheet metal and a heavy base. Friends of animals will forgo use of the foot chain.

choose the right moment. Even when this condition is met, keeping a cockatoo in this fashion is possible only with supervision. Depending on the size and design of its climbing apparatus, every cockatoo will sooner or later begin to explore its surroundings. This can be very detrimental to furniture and other possessions. Trimming the wings is only a partial solution; it helps in those instances where the bird cannot reach the floor by climbing down. Even then, there is no guarantee that the bird will really remain in its proper place all the time.

To ensure this, many "bird lovers" still advocate the outdated tactic of chaining the bird. Chained by one foot to the stand, the bird's freedom of movement is supposed to be limited to a permitted area. Even though the parrot chains still available in the trade today have several swivel joints that are supposed to prevent the chain from twisting, its use is a torture for the animal. Twisted hopelessly around the frame and perch of the stand within minutes, these chains allow the bird no freedom of movement at all. Anyone who has ever seen a cockatoo dangling head downward from its chain will reject this "accessory." The pronounced strain on the chained foot must also be mentioned.

Nowadays, commercially available stands are usually made of metal and offer the advantage— besides hygienic cleanability and the fact that they can hardly be damaged by a parrot's beak —of being equipped with food cups and a tray. On the other hand, the single perch usually does not keep the cockatoo sufficiently occupied. The same is true for the bow perch, which can be a very handy means of transportation. Presupposing the bird's wings have been trimmed, one can unhook it, with the bird still on, and hang it up again in a different place; this way the animal can easily be allowed a sojourn on the terrace or in the garden, for a while.

A climbing tree comes closest to meeting the cockatoo's need for exercise; it is easy to construct one of the desired size and height at home. The simplest way is to set a branch into concrete in a plastic pail; this can be put on a plastic dropcloth. If the branch is replaced often, the health of the bird will benefit from its gnawing on the bark.

Room Aviaries If sufficient room is available in the home, the birds should be offered larger quarters than are offered by a cage. A room aviary is an oversized cage, but this is not what is offered as such in the trade. Usually, commercial "room aviaries" are merely large parrot cages that meet only the minimal requirements. A room aviary takes up a considerable part of the room, with the floor of the room being the floor of the cage and the ceiling its roof. The entire construction must be stable in proportion to its size, but its framework need not be unusually sturdy since it is anchored at floor and ceiling. It goes without saying that wood cannot be used. When selecting the wire mesh, remember to consider the strength and size of the cockatoo's beak.

The construction of ceiling, walls, and floor must be planned with the same considerations in mind. Ceiling tiles are merely objects to satisfy the cockatoo's urge to gnaw; even floor tiles fall victim to the cockatoo's beak, once a dent is made. A lining of asbestos-concrete shingles can be helpful. Outlets and electrical wiring must be particularly well secured. The author knew a pair of Salmon-crested Cockatoos (*C. moluccensis*) that managed again and again to cause short-circuits. Prior to construction, how to clean the room aviary easily must be planned. There must be no hiding places for vermin. If the room will have other uses too, there must be a low wall at least 20 cm. high to reduce dirtying the surroundings.

Whether it will be a breeding or a communal aviary will determine the selection of furnishings. Branches for perching or climbing can be fastened to the wire mesh or mounted on walls and ceiling by means of a wire passing through a drilled hole. Thought should be given not to limit the birds' freedom of movement with an excess of branches. In addition, they should be installed so as to avoid soiling the walls and especially the food and water dishes. For the latter, it is best to use easily cleaned containers that can be set on a feeding table or on the floor. In order to avert fights, the number of dishes should correspond to the number of birds.

Nest boxes are always fastened in the corners of room aviaries, in deference to the animals' need for security. Decorative plants in pots set or hung in the aviary are attractive, but will have a short life span around cockatoos. However, separated from the actual aviary by a plexiglas wall, they can be very effective. The imagination of the bird fancier can be given free rein; a small water basin, for example, or a small artificial brook or waterfall can look very pretty. Nevertheless, practical considerations must always come first. A cockatoo fancier known by the author furnished his beautiful room aviaries with wooden ceilings and a flagstone wall. He was forced to rebuild within a few weeks; the cockatoos gnawed happily on the ceiling and loosened the flagstones after removing the grouting.

Adequate ventilation and lighting for the room aviary must be ensured. A timer switch, possibly combined with a dimmer or at least a night light, will reliably regulate the photoperiod, even when the keeper is absent. Sufficient light is essential for the birds to find their roosts—or their nest boxes during breeding time—even at twilight. It is an advantage if the room itself can be darkened. Especially in summer, all-too-early unwelcome disturbances may thereby be prevented.

Flight Rooms The concept of a flight room describes a room aviary that takes up the entire room; it is another step toward optimal living conditions for the birds. For its construction, the remarks made on room aviaries are essentially valid; here too the matter of cleanability must stay in the foreground. The furnishings also must be planned beforehand; perches and branches for climbing must be fastened accordingly. There are certain things that must be

This stand is 98 cm. high, and the tray measures 60 x 44 cm.

given special consideration. The windows must be protected on the outside by a wire screen; this prevents the birds from escaping in case of broken glass, and it permits the windows to be opened for air. Depending on local conditions – and the next-door neighbors – the windows may be removed entirely during the summer months; they prevent the absorption of ultraviolet rays, so important to the health of the birds. Particularly advantageous for keeping cockatoos is the addition of a wire bay which, even if small, allows the birds an occasional sojourn outdoors. Cockatoos bathe in the rain almost exclusively, which greatly benefits the appearance and growth of the plumage.

Special attention must be given to securing the window frames and sills. If they are not made of marble or metal, they must be protected against cockatoo beaks with sheet-metal strips. Heating also requires our attention; heaters and radiators must be installed so that the animals cannot come into direct contact with the hot parts and get burned. The same safety measures are required for all electrical installations in the flight room. Lamps must be installed so that they cannot be reached by the birds, neither by flying nor by climbing. Electrical wiring is best covered, outlets secured by metal strips, and switches installed outside the room. When fastening metal strips, etc., remember that cockatoos can pull even bolts and screws from the walls.

A vestibule is necessary only if the door leads directly outdoors; cockatoos other than Cockatiels *(N. hollandicus)* generally do not tend to fly in panic, so escape is unlikely when someone enters their room; if the flight room is brighter than the adjoining room, it is most improbable.

Outdoor Aviaries   If breeding is the goal desired by a lover of cockatoos, an outdoor aviary is certainly the best way to house them. Comparable to life in the wild, the requirements of the animals can be met best in this situation. The natural need for exercise is best taken into account here; the sojourn under open skies, at least during the day, has some evident advantages. Cockatoos like to bathe in the rain; in warm weather, this is usually followed by an extensive sunbath. Their supply of vitamin D can be ensured only by unfiltered sunlight.

The size and design of an aviary are limited only by the location and one's purse, apart from the personal tastes of the individual bird fancier. For esthetic reasons, integration of the outdoor aviary into its surroundings should be considered during construction. The location should be chosen to keep the birds as undisturbed by extraneous influences as possible. Breeding cockatoos especially are distinguished by a large measure of sensitivity; unforeseen disturbances usually mean the loss of the brood. The fact that parrots particularly like the morning and the evening sun should also be considered when deciding on the location. Since construction depends on financial ability of the cockatoo owner, only general guidelines are given here.

Although many cockatoos are kept year around, apparently without harm, in only partly covered outdoor aviaries, combining the flight with a suitable shelter room or house is preferable. That all cockatoos are inhabitants of tropical or subtropical regions must not be overlooked. Adapted morphologically and physiologically over thousands of years to a warm climate, the birds' constitution must sooner or later be damaged by our climate. A shelter room warmed in winter provides the necessary protection, particularly since many tropical cockatoo species will breed even during our winter months.

As to the dimensions of the outdoor flight, the same guidelines as always apply: the bigger, the better. For smaller cockatoos, to the size of the Galah *(E. roseicapillus)*, a flight no less than 1 m. wide should be planned; a length of 3 m. appears sufficient. For larger species, such as the White *(C. alba)*, Salmon-crested *(C. moluccensis)*, and particularly the black cockatoos *(Calyptorhynchus spp.)*, this amount of space is insufficient for flight. A width of 1.5– 2.5 m.

fits with a length of 4–8 m. The minimal outdoor-flight height should be 2.0–2.5 m. The animals feel better in larger spaces, but catching an individual becomes a problem.

The framework of the outdoor flight must be made of metal, considering the cockatoo beak; depending on the mesh, material L-shaped or square in section can be used. Rustproof primer is essential and bitumen colors work best; however, galvanizing is preferable. A galvanized framework is maintenance-free; provided with an additional protective coat of paint after one or two years, it is virtually indestructible. It must be pointed out that paint will not adhere to freshly galvanized materials. Frames constructed of aluminum are completely corrosion-resistant, but very expensive.

The size of the wire mesh used depends on the inhabitants of the aviary. While smaller cockatoo species may be kept in spot-welded wire mesh 0.8 mm. square, a White Cockatoo *(C. alba)* will pick apart this kind of mesh in a few hours. In the construction of an aviary for larger species, wavy mesh or steel construction mats must be used. The mesh size usually corresponds closely to the wire gauge. Mesh larger than 12.5 mm. no longer protects against mice and small weasels. With larger mesh sizes, cats and birds of prey can also cause damage, and biting between occupants of adjoining flights is more likely. Double wire mesh, with the finer mesh on the outside, will help to prevent this.

If there is no access to the outdoor flight from the shelter, the necessary doors must be added. They are best located on the front. If several flights are adjoining, the doors from one flight to the next will prevent escape, but getting to the last flight becomes a struggle. Suitably small doors opening inward will reduce the danger of escape to a minimum, if used carefully.

The durability of the wire mesh depends on the wire gauge. A coating with bitumen varnish, applied with a paint roller, increases its life expectancy considerably; here again the metal must first oxidize for several months.

White cockatoos especially are easier to see through mesh painted black, since there is no reflection from the sunlight.

The aviary must have a concrete foundation that extends into the ground for 30 cm. (50 cm. is better), so that rodents, sooner or later attracted by food remnants, are unable to dig their way inside. Since even a 50 cm. foundation does not give absolute protection, additional measures must be taken. Feeding in the shelter room exclusively would be one way. Instead of constructing a concrete apron, it is easier to use concrete border stones, which are available in various thicknesses. The framework of the aviary is bolted to these stones; an air space of 5 mm. between the stones and the framework prevents corrosion in this danger spot.

The rear third of the flight should be covered by a solid roof, so that the animals can take cover in inclement weather. Translucent panels may be used; an extension of about one meter from the shelter room looks best. In the construction of the shelter room, only those materials that can stand up to the bird's beaks, i.e., rocks and bricks, asbestos-concrete, and metal, should be used.

While esthetic considerations play a big part in planning the flight, they should be secondary to functionality in the construction of the shelter. If the space is available, an inside service corridor about 1 m. wide along the shelter rooms offers advantages that cannot be overlooked. The shelter rooms should be constructed so that at least half of each of the walls dividing them is solid, so that one cannot see through them. This prevents disturbances during breeding. Total isolation of the shelter rooms heightens this effect but has the disadvantage that the animals cannot be observed readily from the service corridor and frequently stay shy because of the lack of contact. Therefore the wall toward the service corridor should be made of wire mesh. Once accustomed to their keeper, the animals will barely be disturbed by him.

The hatchway connecting the flight and the shelter should, if possible, be constructed in such a way that it may be opened or closed from outside the aviary. Hatchways situated about 1.2 m. above the ground are quickly found by the birds; dimensions of 20 × 20 cm. minimize heat loss in winter. Sliding doors constructed of asbestos-concrete shingles and wire pulleys allow the hatchways to be opened and closed effortlessly.

Parrots should be trained from the beginning to spend their nights indoors. The advantages are obvious: the danger of losses from predators is reduced, and the birds are not exposed to any disturbances during the night. Their unavoidable noise in the early morning hours will reach the neighbors in somewhat reduced form as well. Accustoming them to the shelter room is simple. If it is illuminated in the evening by a lamp on a timer and if, in addition, the animals are fed in the evening, they will voluntarily go inside at dusk. A perch mounted as high up as possible will be their favorite roost.

Good lighting and ventilation for the shelter room must be provided. Plexiglas panes in the windows reduce the danger of injuries from collisions. To save energy, sufficient insulation is imperative. The guidelines for room aviaries remain valid for furnishing an outdoor aviary, but, especially in the design of the shelter room, considerations of hygiene and functionality must be foremost.

Depending on the size and the inhabitants of the aviary, it may be necessary to protect it with an alarm system. If the outdoor flights are attached to a home, and the birds sheltered inside—a ground-level basement is very suitable for this—then the danger of bird theft, already too common, is reduced. In addition, the construction of a shelter house can be omitted.

Nutrition

The Diet of Wild Cockatoos In the wild, no parrot eats sunflower seeds exclusively. Its menu varies, depending on its range and what is available seasonally. Parrots prefer parts of green plants as far as possible, because they are organically constituted for a limited intake of water. This is especially true for the inhabitants of the steppes of central Australia, which in some cases have to get by on amazingly little water. That precipitation occurs during only a few months presents the animals with severe nutritional and physiological problems. Because of the reduced food supply, they spend the better part of the day foraging; they eat anything that appears edible. The bulk of their diet consists of seeds of all kinds, eaten green, half-ripe, or ripe, depending on the stage of vegetation. In their search for food, they do not neglect the farmers' grain fields; this explains their usually low popularity with this segment of the population. If hundreds of cockatoos band together during their seasonal travels and attack a grain field, nothing but devastation remains behind. They can also do a great deal of damage to orchards. They like to eat fruit, often consuming only a small part, especially of the larger kinds, and then throwing the rest carelessly to the ground. Even green leaves are picked off and chewed or dropped. When the availability of food is limited, the juicy bark of twigs adds welcome variety to the menu. In addition to the basic nutrients (proteins, fats, and carbohydrates), an organism requires a number of important minerals and trace elements; these requirements are met in this way. Eating bits of rotting or charred wood is also helpful.

Depending on the availability of food and the competition of other species, some cockatoo species have evolved toward nutritional specialization. By occupying an ecological niche, they are not competing with other bird species. The ecological niche constitutes, in a way, the "occupation" of an animal species, whereby the concept refers not only to the habitat but also describes the specific circumstances in which this species interacts with its environment. Along with territoriality, it offers another possibility for avoiding competition. Thus, a nectar-feeding lory and a cockatoo will never get in each other's way, since the basics of their lives are too different. On the other hand, this explains why only a few cockatoo species coexist in the same range. According to the Darwinian principle of natural selection, only the best-adapted individuals survive; therefore certain morphological adaptations must develop parallel to feeding behavior.

Above all, this concerns the shape of the beak and the structure of the tongue as the most important organs for feeding. The interrelation of beak construction and feeding have been pointed out repeatedly. Caring for specialized feeders as the Gang-gang Cockatoo (C. fimbriatum) presents us with considerable problems. In the wild, this beautiful cockatoo feeds almost exclusively on the seeds of the peppermint eucalyptus, which are about the size of a grain of millet. Since the kernels are accessible only with difficulty because of their hard hulls, the animals spend almost the entire day feeding. This explains why this species in particular tends toward feather plucking in aviaries. In addition to certain deficiencies, boredom surely plays a big part.

Even those cockatoo species that live in the tropical rain forests—these are characterized by more constant vegetational conditions—do not find the same food selection the year around, in all seasons. In addition to fruit, oil-containing seeds are the chief constituent of their diet.

Since their table is usually more richly set, we find no such clearly defined specialized feeders among the inhabitants of tropical islands.

To summarize, the principle of nutritional variety applies to all cockatoo species. Their requirements for basic nutrients, vitamins, minerals, and trace elements can be met only in this manner. In the wild, the animals are in a position to select the food that meets a particular need. There are frequent reports of cockatoos that fulfill their requirement for animal protein by eating insect larvae. These are skillfully picked out of rotting wood with the beak. Parrots kept in human care, on the other hand, depend on the knowledge and care of their keeper for their nutrition. Most often, their diet is much too one-sided; that they nevertheless appear more or less healthy testifies to their undemanding and hardy constitutions. However, this partially explains the comparatively low rate of success in breeding them.

Nutrition in Captivity: Seed Cockatoos are seed eaters without exception; seeds such as millet, canary, our domestic grains, sunflower seed, and various nuts are the main staples of their diet. The value of a food depends on its quality, i.e., its nutrient and energy content and its digestibility, which can be determined only by chemical analyses and scientific feeding experiments. These values are available on food labels and permit direct quality comparisons. The seeds under consideration for feeding cockatoos can conveniently be put into two groups: those rich in carbohydrates and those high in fats. In addition to our domestic grains, various kinds of millet belong to the first group; this is a collective name for several botanical genera. Our domestic grains are rich in carbohydrates (50–70%), in which the main nutritive vlaue comes from plant starch, a nutrient made of many sugar units. The average protein content is around 10–12%; this is found mainly in the aleuronic layer and the sprout. The same is true of the raw-fat content, which usually does not exceed 2–5%. The raw-fiber content varies with the proportion of spelts and is less, therefore, in hulled seeds than in unhulled. Hulls and spelts are particularly hard to digest. The mineral content of domestic grains is minimal. In their ripe state, the seeds listed are only reluctantly eaten by cockatoos. Mixed with commercial parrot food, even kernels of corn are usually ignored. It is different when the seeds are fed in a half-ripe or sprouted state. The milky seed heads of wheat especially are gladly accepted by all cockatoos; offering them also helps to meet the animals' need for occupation. Half-ripe ears of corn top the animals' list of favorites and are especially suitable for the acclimation of newly imported animals or for feeding sick birds that refuse all other foods. A stock of this, laid in late summer and kept in the freezer, is often extremely useful. Although all the kinds of millet available here—they come to us predominantly from the earth's warmer zones—have small seeds, they are eaten happily by cockatoos. Their nutrient content is about the same as that of domestic grains; because of their low raw-fiber content, digestibility is very high. In feeding cockatoos it is best to use the commercial millet mixtures, since the seeds contained in them are of sufficient quality and are more advantageously priced than are separate kinds. These seed mixtures usually also contain some canary, which is also gladly taken. If a so-called large-parrot mix without sunflower seed is fed, it very frequently also contains buckwheat and rape; the former especially gets a good response. The pumpkin seeds, on the other hand, are frequently ignored. Rice, even unhulled, is usually not to the taste of cockatoos, but when cooked it is particularly suitable for sick or young birds.

Of the oil seeds, sunflower seed is the most important in feeding cockatoos. Either white, black, or striped kinds are available here; the color as a rule is no indicator of quality. Sunflower seed contains about 20% raw protein and 5–6% carbohydrate in addition to a fat content of 50–55%; the composition of the protein is usually better than in cereal seeds. Their mineral content is also particularly high. Because of the high fat content, sunflower seed should not amount to more than 50% of the diet. As a substitute, feeding teazle, which the animals like very much, is recommended. In general, habit seems to play a big role, especially with cockatoos. Being stubborn animals, they will often ignore striped or dark sunflower seeds once they are accustomed to white ones, even though they are identical in flavor and composition. Hemp seed, which all cockatoo species like to eat, should be used only sparingly in a parrot diet. If its proportion in the food mixture is too high, it is not tolerated well by the birds. Peanuts, which belong to the legume family, are especially popular with all parrots; however, they should be offered carefully because of their high fat content. The same is true for such nuts as hazelnuts, walnuts, brazil nuts, and cembra nuts, which, given as a special treat, are particularly useful to entice aviary birds into the shelter room in the evening. The proportion of nuts fed depends on the size of the bird; it can be commensurately higher with large cockatoo species. Mung beans, which are also a legume, are eaten only in the sprouted state.

Chemical Composition of the Foods Most Commonly Fed to Parrots

(Values indicate percentage of dry weight and may vary because of quality and storage time)

	Raw Protein	Raw Fat	Raw Fiber	Carbohydrate	Ash
Sunflower seed, hulled	20.2	54.5	4.0	5.9	2.5
Peanuts, hulled	26.0	43.5	5.2	11.2	2.3
Hemp	22.6	30.2	11.9	19.5	3.9
Pumpkin seed	26.8	35.0	17.6	5.6	3.5
Niger	18.2	40.4	13.5	12.7	3.3
Teazle, unhulled	14.3	27.8	31.2	16.5	3.0
Millet	12.3	3.8	9.1	59.1	3.7
Spray millet	11.7	4.2	7.4	61.7	3.0
Oats	11.4	4.8	19.5	58.3	3.2
Wheat	10.8	1.7	2.6	71.3	1.7
Corn	9.4	4.1	2.4	70.6	1.5
Paddy rice	8.5	2.1	8.7	63.2	5.4
Buckwheat	11.4	2.5	12.3	58.7	3.1
Canary seed	14.9	5.5	8.9	52.3	6.2
Mung beans	21.4	1.7	4.4	57.5	3.6
Rowan berries	1.1	1.5	2.7	20.1	0.6
Carrot	1.2	0.2	1.1	9.4	1.0
Apple	0.3	0.3	2.3	13.5	0.4
Brewer's yeast	47.5	2.0	0.9	31.6	8.0
Farmer's cheese	27.7	1.5	–	5.7	1.2
Ground shrimp	41.4	6.7	–	11.1	28.8

In addition to those listed, the following seeds and fruits may be fed, as their seasonal availability permits: lettuce, thistle, mullein, evening primrose, orach, plantain, fir, and spruce, and also birch and oak. Many seeds are preferred in their half-ripe state. Thus, cockatoos prefer green hazelnuts to ripe nuts. Even many kinds of millet are liked better in their milky-ripe state, so that cultivation of the hardier species of millet in our climate is worthwhile.

In addition to internal quality, external quality—namely cleanliness, freshness, and absence of infestation by parasites and microorganisms—has considerable significance. Oil-containing foods especially tend to become rancid during prolonged storage. Before feeding newly purchased supplies, oil seeds should be checked for this by a taste test. Rancid foods may cause serious health disturbances. The same is true of moldy-smelling food, which is often infested by *Aspergillus* fungi; serious and even fatal poisoning is not a rare consequence. Proper storage of the food in a dry, dark room can help in prevention. Of course, this applies less to cockatoos kept singly in the home than to a large number of animals kept in an aviary. All seeds should be offered in smooth, easily cleanable food dishes, in which the smaller seeds are mixed. It is better to offer the larger seeds separately, as the amount eaten can be monitored and controlled better this way. When feeding half-ripe seeds, the food dishes have to be cleaned more often.

Sprouts Freshly sprouted seeds are an excellent food, especially prior to and during breeding, since with sprouting the stored nutrients are enzymatically altered in ways nutritionally important for the bird's constitution. This entails a nutrient loss of 20%; it is consumed by the sprout itself. Sprouted seed must be prepared with meticulous care; otherwise, it can become an ideal growth medium for disease germs.

As sprouts for cockatoos, sunflower seed and our domestic grains are particularly suitable.

The proportions of the mixture should be adjusted seasonally. Grain sprouts are especially rich in vitamin E, the so-called fertility vitamin, so that they are an excellent conditioning food at the start of the breeding season. At this time the proportion of oats should be relatively high, but it should be replaced by sprouted wheat during the period of rearing young. Outside the breeding season, only sprouted sunflower seed is given.

Correctly done, preparing sprouted seed is no trouble. First, the seeds are carefully washed in a fine strainer to remove disease germs and fungus spores, and dust and dirt as well. Then the seed is soaked for twenty-four hours in a plastic container filled with water. During this time the seeds absorb the amount of water necessary for germination. Then the seeds are rinsed in a sieve until the water runs off clear and clean. If the seeds remain in this sieve for another twenty-four hours with repeated rinsing and stirring, they will have reached the stage of sprouting that is best for feeding. The speed of germination depends on temperature. If the correct stage of germination is missed—when the root is only a few millimeters long—the sprouts will be accepted only reluctantly or not at all by the cockatoos. Sprouts that smell moldy or sour must not be fed. Sprouting seeds on foam or in so-called sprouters encourages the growth of disease germs, unless the strictest cleanliness is maintained.

It is even simpler in outdoor aviaries to just rake various seeds into the ground. The savanna-dwelling cockatoos especially like to find their food on the ground and gladly seize this opportunity. For this reason, the author prefers an earth floor to a concrete floor in the aviary, although this has hygienic disadvantages without a doubt. Cleanliness and several annual bacteriological and parasitological tests of the droppings reduce the risk.

Green Foods That feeding green food plays a considerable role in keeping cockatoos is proved by the fact that in an aviary filled with cockatoos usually not a single blade of grass will be allowed to grow. This is especially true for those species that prefer to find their food on the ground. Even the roots of sprouting weeds are dug up and eaten by Galahs *(E. roseicapillus)*.

In first place, there is chickweed *(Stellaria media)*, which can be found the year around, with the exception of periods of hard frost. As with the equally suitable shepherd's purse *(Capsella bursa-pastoris)*, dandelion *(Taraxarum officinale)*, and plantain *(Plantago)*, not only are the leaves eaten, but the seed heads also are consumed with great enthusiasm.

When collecting weeds, it is best to follow a guide book obtainable at a bookstore, or one's own observations; wild seeds and green food eaten by our native bird species are almost always suitable for feeding our exotic charges. Special attention must be paid to the place where the weeds are collected. Greens polluted by insecticides or herbicides have caused heavy losses to bird owners. Even careful washing offers little help, since the poisons are stored in the plant itself. Many apparently infertile clutches are undoubtedly the result of this.

Chard, lettuce, and spinach are also suitable green foods, because – like native weeds – they contain many important vitamins and trace elements. Here too, extreme care in selection is required, because store-bought lettuce has almost always been sprayed. Growing greens at home is the safest solution, although this is not always possible. Leaf lettuce is especially suitable; however, an excess of lettuce can lead to intestinal disturbances.

Fresh buds and leaves of unsprayed fruit trees, and of alders, lilacs, elders, and willows may also be given. They are rich in important minerals and trace elements and are gladly eaten, as is their bark.

Fruits, Vegetables, Berries All cockatoos should be given fruit daily to supplement their diet. Unaccustomed to this, the animals often turn it down initially. Patience will almost always achieve the goal and will be rewarded

by the birds' good condition. Next to greens, fruits are particularly rich in vitamins. All kinds are suitable for feeding, and the range need not be limited, since tomatoes, cucumbers, and celery are welcome. There are no limits to the inventiveness of the cockatoo owner; he will soon find out which kinds are preferred. Offered in small, cut-up pieces in glazed food dishes, everything is usually eaten; if larger pieces are spiked onto a nail, most of it drops to the ground and is wasted. Such bite-sized pieces can easily be mixed with additional vitamin-and-mineral mixtures or, if necessary, with medicines.

Cockatoos enjoy root vegetables such as carrots, comfrey, and kohlrabi, but vegetables of the cabbage family are also accepted. Some animals will even eat cooked potatoes.

When collecting and feeding wild berries, once again it is best to be guided by the behavior of our native birds. Any berries eaten by them are edible for all cockatoos. In first place are the fruits of the rowan, hawthorn, and firethorn, which ripen in early August. The flesh as well as the seeds of the fruit are eaten. Rose-hips of the various kinds of roses are also enjoyed. Berries of all kinds may be given fresh, or they may be dried and stored. Freezing them is best, however; this way, the birds' diet can be enriched even in winter.

In feeding fruit, vegetables, and berries, the same precautions must be taken as when feeding greens. Careful washing and peeling, if necessary, will prevent sickness. In those fruits that are grown for their decorative value, the low vitamin content is often outweighed by a high toxicity.

Foods of Animal Origin Foods of animal origin are distinguished by a high content of valuable protein that cannot be supplied by other dietary items. Cockatoos require them in large proportions; lack of them is often evident in poor condition, abnormal molting, and susceptibility to disease.

Animal foods play a large role for cockatoos in

the wild, and the requirement for them is met by consuming insects in all stages of development. For this reason, it does not seem advisable to do without such valuable additions to the diet. The hunger with which many parrots gnaw on raw bones and eat cheese or yogurt indicates their need for such nutrients; these items contribute in considerable measure to maintain health and increase vitality in our charges.

On the other hand, the method of feeding these foods often causes difficulties for the bird owner. Insects, especially the mealworm larvae often used in the care of birds, are not suitable for cockatoos because of their hard and heavy chitin covering; usually they are not accepted anyway. Meat of soft consistency is also refused, and the danger of spoilage is too great. Large bones that contain marrow seem to be more suitable, since they are busily gnawed on by cockatoos of all species; sometimes they are cracked and the marrow eaten. Cubes of hard cheese are also taken gladly. This requires sensitivity on the part of the keeper. An excessive taste for cheese may lead to clumps of casein in the crop and so to serious digestive problems.

Eggs occupy a central position in feeding birds. Hard-boiled, chopped eggs are highly valuable, since the egg, the nutritional reservoir for the growing chick, contains all essential nutrients and other elements. Still, in feeding eggs, the danger of transmitting fowl typhus (*Salmonella*) or leukosis cannot be completely excluded. Although egg yolk is rich in vitamins, minerals, and trace elements, it must not be given daily, since it is hard to digest and in large amounts may lead to illness. Egg-white poisoning because of feeding egg white excessively has also been known.

Dried shrimp is also a good protein-and-mineral food. When purchasing, watch out for differences in quality.

Recently, supplemental feeding of parrots with dog and cat foods has been popularized. The author tested many commercially available foods and was especially successful with dry cat food. All cockatoo species offered this accepted

it readily after a short familiarization period. Ground and mixed with fruit, it is usually eaten right away. The danger of spoilage with this kind of food is virtually nonexistent.

Ground beef heart, mixed with bread crumbs into a crumbly mass, is avidly consumed, particularly in the breeding season. It need not be stressed that foods of animal provenance must be fresh daily and prepared with special care.

Minerals In order to ensure a complete diet, additional minerals may be mixed with the food, because minerals, such as calcium, phosphorus, and sodium, and the trace elements iron, manganese, copper, and zinc are of great importance for the functioning of a bird's constitution. A suitably varied diet reduces the danger of mineral deficiency but does not absolutely guarantee sufficiency. For this purpose, the possibilities range from expensive preparations for human medicine and those used in the nutrition of babies to edible calcium and grit. As powder, sprinkled over fruit and sprouts, calcium or grit are readily accepted. Oyster-shell and mineral blocks fulfill the same purpose in supplying minerals, but are not always accepted. Because of the danger of transmitting diseases, ground eggshells should not be fed.

Charcoal and charred wood are rich in minerals, and cockatoos like to gnaw on them. If the birds are frequently given fresh twigs, which will be chewed eagerly, not only is the birds' need for occupation met, but this also supplies mineral salts. Wood is rich in trace elements and additionally contains such important organic compounds as saponin, pectin, and various tannins and alkaloids.

Even feeding fresh forest loam and river sand contributes to the mineral supply. Ingestion of sand and small pebbles has another nutritional and physiological significance; these act as grindstones for food in the ventriculus.

Vitamins Vitamins are substances that as a rule cannot be synthesized by animals and people; instead they must be ingested with food, since they are essential for many metabolic processes and indispensible for growth and reproduction. Plants are the source of vitamins. They contain the chemical building blocks, the so-called pro-vitamins, which are transformed into the actual vitamins in the bodies of animals and humans. For instance, the carotenoids richly present in carrots are transformed into vitamin A by some liver enzymes. Vitamin deficiency always causes serious metabolic disorders; a complete absence of vitamins is called avitaminosis. This is often caused by poor proportions in the composition of the diet. At most, parrots with a varied diet need additional vitamins during the winter months or during the breeding season. Thus

A Salmon-crested Cockatoo (C. moluccensis) enjoys eating a pear.

fertility may be increased considerably by measured doses of vitamin E before the breeding season.

Recently, more and more synthetic vitamin preparations, mixtures of all the essential vitamins, have become available. Those in powder form are preferable. Some vitamins are not water-soluble; in addition, adding vitamins to the drinking water seems futile in view of the low drinking requirements of cockatoos especially. A multivitamin in powder form can be stored longer and can easily be administered by sprinkling it over fruit and vegetables. The strong odor of vitamin B_1 is usually not annoying in this form. The vitamin preparations used in human medicine can also be used in the care of birds. They contain all essential vitamins, such as vitamins A, B_1, B_2, B_6, B_{12}, pantothenic acid, C, D_2, niacin, and E. Since there is a danger of overdoses of vitamins A and D especially, a veterinarian should be consulted before they are used.

Rearing Foods Many authors suggest the use of additional rearing foods during the breeding period. The secret recipes go from soaked bread to complicated mixes that are guarded by the breeder like a precious treasure. While some substances certainly qualify as stimulants before the breeding season, the author is of the opinion that a special rearing food as such is unnecessary. A cockatoo fed a broad and varied diet will select from the foods offered those which are suitable for the age and stage of development of the nestlings. Only the average amounts of foods consumed need to be changed during the breeding period. Many cockatoos alter their feeding habits during breeding and will eat things they refused before. It is up to the sensitivity of the bird fancier to detect these things. That the food must be especially rich in nutrients, vitamins, and minerals during the breeding period goes without saying. The better and more varied the diet, the more successful breeding will be, and the stronger and more vital the offspring.

Above: Galahs (*E. r. assimilis*) are followers of cultivation. Here they are looking for seeds on a road traveled by trucks carrying grain.
Right: Major Mitchell's Cockatoos *(C. leadbeateri)* in a tree hollow.

Care

Grooming and Feather Trimming Besides appropriate feeding, regular care and grooming also contribute to the well-being of parrots kept in human care. A healthy parrot, kept as a bird of its species should be, can be recognized by its smooth, immaculate plumage, among other things. Cockatoos in particular spend a good part of the day caring for their feathers. The feathers are pulled through the beak and any soiling is cleaned off. By means of the oily dust of the powder downs, the plumage is oiled and kept pliable. Although the animals do most of the work, their keeper must help with some basic needs. Like all large parrots, cockatoos must be given a shower at least once a week. This satisfies their natural need for bathing. In the wild, they prefer to bathe in the rain. At the same time, the regular soaking guarantees healthy growth of the feathers; it helps to keep the vanes of the wing and tail feathers tight. Another point that cannot be overlooked is the fact that cockatoos are very dusty. To the dismay of the housewife, the powder-down dust covers not only the plumage of the bird, but after a short time—this is especially true for the larger cockatoo species—all the furniture in the room is also covered with the oily white feather dust. Regular showers will help at least temporarily. If the bird is not tame, it is best to use a mister of the type used for house plants. The animals usually enjoy this shower so much, once their initial shyness is overcome, that they assume an open-winged posture to get a uniform soaking.

Tame cockatoos may be taken into the shower in the wire part of their cages or on a stand; here they are showered with lukewarm water. During warm weather they may also be showered outdoors with a garden hose. If they are kept in an aviary, a sprinkler system should by all means be installed. The simplest method is to put a perforated garden hose atop the flight. Opening of the faucet—early morning or late afternoon are particularly good times—produces the unique performance of "rainbathing" cockatoos, hanging head downward on the wire mesh. It goes without saying that, just as for a shower indoors, a sufficiently warm water temperature must be maintained. A cockatoo kept in this manner requires an additional bathing dish only when breeding. At this time bathing is less important for grooming, but serves instead to supply the clutch with the required ambient humidity.

If the cockatoo is to be kept loose in the home, its wing feathers may be trimmed in order to reduce the danger of escape. While cockatoos with untrimmed wings are truly acrobatic fliers, a cockatoo with its wings clipped—unlike amazons, cockatoos never entirely stop attempting to fly—will become a threat to any furniture in the vicinity of the cage. In any case, whether to trim the feathers should be carefully weighed, because, once done, it takes two years for them to grow back completely.

If, nevertheless, the decision to clip has been made, it is best to have someone experienced do it. It is best to trim the secondaries and the inner primaries of both wings; with wings closed, the trimming will not be evident. The wings of new imports are usually trimmed, though with little expertise, because this considerably facilitates handling the animals during transport. Trimming only one wing is fundamentally unwise, because if the animal still tries to fly, it will not be able to keep its balance and will fall sideways or head-over-heels. Before a trimmed cockatoo is taken on an excursion to the terrace or the garden, the extent of the trim and flight ability remaining must be checked in the room. A sound middle ground must be found, which on one hand prevents the bird's escape but on the other does not cause it to drop like a stone to the ground at the first attempt to fly. Even for an occasional stay outdoors, the condition of the wings must be checked frequently. Many a bird fancier who trimmed his bird's wings shortly before the main molt ends up looking for his pet in the lost-and-found ads in a few weeks.

Trimming the Claws and Beak If the cockatoo is kept in a cage, it often happens that its claws grow faster than they wear down. This increases the danger that the animal will catch its overgrown claws in the wire mesh and hurt itself. In addition, the needle-sharp claws of a tame bird can cause painful scratches on the keeper's skin. A "natural nail file" can help here; its construction has been mentioned in the section on cages. Overgrown claws must be cut; for this it is best to use a nail clipper. Part of a bird's claw is living tissue; the growth zone at its base is well supplied with blood. Accordingly, clipping must be done extremely cautiously. Also, as the claw is not translucent as in small birds and the blood vessel cannot be seen, one must make an estimation. It is best to have the bird held firmly by another person; in this manner, unforeseen movements and injuries are prevented. The place to cut is shown in the illustration. If, despite all precautions, there should be some bleeding, it must be stopped with a blood-clotting medicine. Afterwards, the bird should be left completely alone, because excessive agitation leads to increased blood loss. Many bird fanciers prefer to have someone else cut their pet's claws since the bird may resent the procedure; one can frighten his own bird this way. In any case, it is best to secure expert help, unless one is completely sure of the correct procedure.

All this is true as well for trimming the beak. Overgrown mandibles, growths on them, and other abnormalities are usually rooted in metabolic abnormalities. In addition to the cosmetic remedy, in each case diet and accommodations should be re-evaluated.

Temperature and Humidity The location of the cage is also important. Care should always be taken to keep one's pet out of drafts. Cockatoos, though not susceptible to cool temperatures, tend to catch cold if exposed to drafts. When building a room aviary or a flight room, thought must be given to ventilating it without causing drafts. The same is true for aviaries; if the hatchway to the outdoor flight is at medium height, the animals perch out of a draft at night even with it open. Sufficient ventilation is essential in all cases, because only a good supply of oxygen guarantees unimpeded functoning of the body's metabolism. Like all birds, cockatoos do not like overheated, smoky rooms. Since they are not sensitive to low temperatures, a winter temperature of 6–8 C. can be considered sufficient. When the animals begin to breed, the temperature must be raised. Of course, a parrot kept at room temperature must not be set into a barely heated bird house without the necessary acclimation. For humidity to be sufficient, it should never be less than 60%. Inhabitants of tropical rain forests have their own special requirements.

Hygiene Next in importance to the daily ration of food and water is hygiene. Cages should be cleaned at least once a week and furnished with a fresh layer of sand. Special attention should be given to the perches, which should be cleaned more often since they become soiled with droppings. The water dishes are a veritable playground for germs. With insufficient cleaning, algae and fungal slime soon grow, transforming the drinking water into a foul brew. In aviaries, seed hulls and droppings are best removed with a soft leaf rake. How often cleaning is needed depends on the number of inhabitants and the size of the flight. Feeding only in the shelter room saves a lot of trouble. A layer of river sand must be changed regularly, and the earth in the outdoor flight

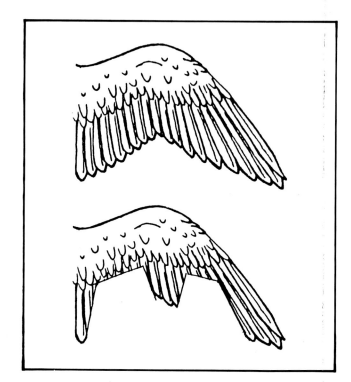

Above: Ducorps's Cockatoo (*C. ducorpsii*) preening.
Below: Claws may be shortened to their normal length only if they are really too long (right). Even when trimming only the tip (left), care must be taken so that the blood vessel is not injured.

Above: With feathers trimmed as shown here, the animal's freedom of movement is greatly restricted, but because the outer primaries remain uncut, the wing still looks intact, at least in the resting position.
Below: Sulphur-crested Cockatoo (*C. g. triton*) preening.

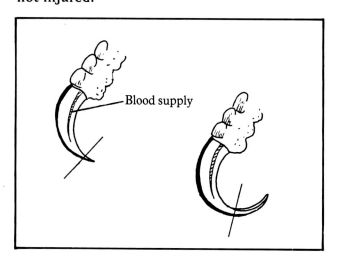

Blood supply

Major Mitchell's Cockatoo (*C. l. leadbeateri*)
leaving the nesting cavity. These animals
prefer tall trees near watercourses.
Photographed near Lake Hindmarsh, Victoria.

must be turned over to a good depth at least twice a year. If the cockatoos have contact with wild birds, bacteriological and parasitological tests of the droppings by an animal-health laboratory twice a year is recommended. Particularly susceptible are the savanna-dwelling species, as they like to forage on the ground.

Illness A discussion of this topic is purposely avoided here; a detailed discussion would go beyond the scope of this book anyway. Instead, the pertinent literature should be consulted, because too often hasty measures do more harm than good. The treatment of ill birds should be left to experienced persons; even for a small-animal veterinarian, avian medicine may be a difficult field. Particularly if the sick bird is a specimen almost impossible to replace, it is best to make every effort to get the advice of a bird specialist from a veterinary school.

If the overall condition of the patient permits, a sample of its droppings should be sent to an animal-health laboratory for testing, before beginning any medical treatment. Appropriate therapy is possible only after bacteriological and parasitological tests and, if results are positive, susceptibility tests have been done. Any other treatment is a kind of gamble; countless parrots with liver damage or an infestation of endoparasites, for instance, have been "treated" to death with useless antibiotics.

Administering medicine is an additional stress to the weakened organism and requires especial sensitivity. On the other hand, many animals can be saved by the correct medicine, once their disease is correctly diagnosed. This way, through one's experiences, the number of losses due to illness can be kept down, even in a large stock.

It must be noted that antibiotic treatment, once begun, must be continued for a certain period, and the dosage must be correct. Even when the bird appears to be healthy again, it still may be a carrier of disease germs, which may become resistant if the treatment ends prematurely. The treatment for endoparasites must be repeated after some days or weeks, since the active ingredients usually fail to affect the larval stages of the parasites. Specifically discouraged is a daily dose of antibiotics to increase the bird's resistance to disease; this will lead to diametrically opposed results. A commentary on "Diseases of Parrots" by Dr. Manfred Heidenreich, a practicing veterinarian and director of the bird clinic at the veterinary school in Hannover, Germany, has been published as part of *Handbook of Lovebirds* by Horst Bielfeld.

Taming A cockatoo kept singly sooner or later will bring joy to its owner only if it is tame. Though poor talkers, these parrots are in demand chiefly because they tame easily. The owner of a tame bird must be aware of the responsibility toward the animal which he has taken on. As social beings, cockatoos lacking natural mates become very close to their keepers, but unlike tame Grey Parrots or amazons, they usually accept any person as a mate substitute. Accordingly, such an animal suffers if it is neglected. If one cannot spare the necessary time, one should forgo taming, if not keeping, a cockatoo altogether.

Taming is comparatively simple, if a few things are taken into consideration. They first come up when purchasing a cockatoo. If it is possible to buy a tame, hand-reared bird, it will surely prove to be a particularly lovable pet before long. Animals that arrive tame were, as a rule, taken from their nests in their home ranges before fledging and reared by hand. The resulting tameness is a misimprinting, with all the concomitant disadvantages. Instead of a bird of the same species, it learns to think of a human as its mate. All social behavior is irreversibly directed toward him. For this reason, such an animal is permanently unsuitable for breeding; exceptions prove the rule and depend on the degree of imprinting. On the other hand, such a cockatoo is especially affectionate toward the human and, if one has the necessary time, gives much pleasure. The fact that these birds often prefer women keepers derives from the fact that in the countries of origin, rearing the nestlings is usually women's work. Since natural fear is lacking, they also become close to men quite rapidly and forget the bad experiences they had with men on their way to Europe. Their strong social needs predominate. In general, a bird purchased young becomes tame more quickly than an older cockatoo does.

Once the newly purchased bird gets home, it should be given a few days for acclimation. Only after the animal has familiarized itself with its new surroundings may one begin to make contact with it. This begins with quiet encouragement in the course of daily feedings; broadly speaking, one should move quietly and calmly when near the new pet. When the cockatoo no longer flutters excitedly during the necessary daily chores in and around the cage, one may attempt to gain its trust. The bird will soon associate favorite tidbits such as peanuts and fruit with the hand of the keeper; this is a decisive step on the path to taming. Until now, most of the experiences connected with the human hand were negative; the frequent captures during transport, quarantine, and sale make long-lasting impressions. However, sooner or later, every cockatoo will overcome this entirely natural fear, because it needs the contact. Once this step is taken, the next becomes easier. Since social grooming is part of the behavior of all species of cockatoos, it offers a way to foster trust. The first place to attempt scratching should always be the base of the beak. Once the animal realizes that the scratching hand presents no danger, it will soon allow its nape feathers to be scratched. Since in a natural cockatoo relationship, grooming is not limited to the area of the head, one may easily work around by way of the back and the breast to the vicinity of the feet. Only when this has been achieved, may one attempt to accustom the cockatoo to the hand.

Usually one can allow supervised excursions outside the cage before this time. At the beginning, trimmed wings are frequently helpful in taming, because an unclipped parrot often will try to save itself by flying. If the bird has gone astray fluttering, it should never be recaptured by hand; it is best to put the wire part of the cage, which is removable in modern models, over the bird. Otherwise, trust painstakingly acquired can too easily be lost again.

In the same manner, a gloved hand will frighten the bird, reawakening negative experiences of capture and transport. Generally, one should avoid anything which might lead to a loss of trust during this phase. If one is really forced to capture or restrain the animal, it is best to leave this to another person or to quickly wrap the cockatoo in a towel so that it cannot see anything.

As the first step in hand-taming a parrot, many authors list accustoming the bird to a stick, which is, as it were, put under it. In the opinion of the author, this is not necessary. When touched on the belly, parrots usually instinctively move a foot toward the hand, and it can be touched and moved with the fingers. Once the cockatoo is accustomed to this, it is only a small step to give the foot a gentle tug and get the bird to climb onto the hand. As always, gentle, soft encouragement and small rewards by way of tidbits or social grooming will help. If an animal bites out of fear at first, it is simply not ready for the hand; even gentle taps will not accomplish this. On the other hand, tame cockatoos must be reprimanded sometimes, because young tame animals especially are often known to exhibit rude manners. Such animals usually do not resent a gentle tap.

No parrot can be more charming than a really tame cockatoo; one can take advantage of the natural playfulness of young animals to teach them all kinds of tricks. Although this is usually not what the animal would do on its own, at least it prevents the possibility of boredom. Once a cockatoo is tame, when its keeper is nearby, it will make a fuss in its cage until the door is opened. Ofttimes its affection can become annoying; however, this must be realized well in advance.

Facing page: White cockatoo *(C. alba),* 82 days old.

Right: Sulphur-crested Cockatoo (*C. g. fitzroyi*) in the eucalyptus savannah in northern Australia, near Darwin.
Below: Emerging feather sheaths on a White Cockatoo (*C. alba*).

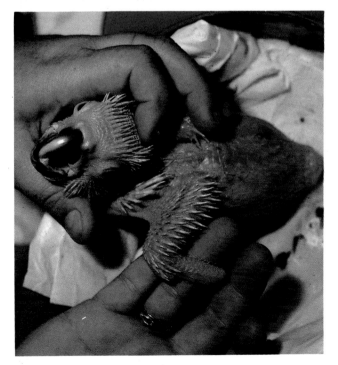

Breeding

With the exception of the Cockatiel *(N. hollandicus)*, one does not frequently find reports of successful cockatoo breeding. The Cockatiel may already be considered to be domesticated; the term *domestication* describes a process by which an animal gradually changes from a wild creature into a pet. By altering living conditions, i.e., the diet or influencing mate selection, man replaces natural selection with an artificial selection done according to certain guidelines. This brings about morphological and physiological changes; breeding various color varieties is an example. But changes resulting from artificial selection may be observed even in behavior; a reduction of instinctive behavior is often a consequence. Such animals frequently breed without difficulties, their basic needs satisfied. On the other hand, evidence of degeneration may be observed, not only in physical characteristics but also in behavior patterns. Bad qualities are also hereditary; inbreeding strengthens such traits in the animals' genotype. In the breeding strains developed this way, the instinctive relationships between mates or between parents and young no longer function; aberrations in breeding are a natural consequence. Many Australian parakeet species are excellent examples of this. To apply this to the cockatoos—which are almost without exception wild-caught—means that if, under favorable conditions, the animals proceed to breed, it usually works without a hitch. Accordingly, many authors do not consider the propagation of cockatoos to be particularly difficult. So, the question becomes this: What are favorable conditions?

Preparations Putting together pairs for breeding requires special attention. Since sexual dimorphism is pronounced in almost all species, it is easy to select a pair; however, this is by no means a breeding pair. As noted before, cockatoos live in a "monogamous marriage," just like all other parrot species, and mates often choose one another before sexual maturity. During this "engagement period," behaviors of the reproduction cluster are practiced freely. Thus, in many parrot species, attempts at copulation may be observed long before sexual maturity. In cockatoos, this occurs between three and five years of age, depending on the species. The conclusions that a breeder can draw from the above statements are simple: the younger the animals, the more promising a forced pairing will be. If there is enough space and money, one should purchase several animals at once; this way mates can choose one another.

As markedly social beings, even arbitrarily paired cockatoos appear to get along well with each other in most cases; this is evident to the keeper by behavior such as social grooming. That this is often nothing more than a lowering of the provocation threshold is proved by the fact that an unpaired cockatoo will sooner or later attach itself to a human. Such a relationship cannot be called successful, no more than the "pairing" of two animals of the same sex can. Two cockatoos of the same sex, once accustomed to each other, will often preen each other; even attempts at copulation are frequently observed. In these cases the dominant animal assumes the role of the male.

If a pair are really compatible, all other factors play only a subordinate role. Sufficient room, optimal nesting facilities, and good care heighten the likelihood of successful breeding, but if the animals are really in a breeding mood, they will often accept quite adverse circumstances. Since most cockatoo marriages in captivity are not based on "affection" but on a lack of other choices, it is wise to make all external conditions as favorable as possible. The chances for successful breeding are increased considerably. The topics treated in the sections on care, feeding, and housing offer important guidelines here.

A planned diet can work as a stimulus. In the wild, cockatoos do not find the same food the year around; food is subject to seasonal changes. Only when they find conditions favorable will they proceed to breed. These rhythmically changing conditions should be duplicated in captivity. Several weeks before the beginning of the breeding season, the diet should be altered accordingly. The proportion of fruit, sprouts, and animal protein is now increased. Grain sprouts are especially rich in vitamin E, which has a favorable influence on the activity of the gonads and the maturation of the egg cells. If necessary, this vitamin may be mixed with the food. However, this requires a certain amount of care, because it may lead to bloody fights, especially if only one of the two partners is sexually mature. More than one cockatoo cock in breeding condition, thus stimulated, has injured or even killed his younger female mate. The defeated animal must be able to escape, or the abilities of the ardent lover must be limited by carefully trimming his wings. On the other hand, after the full molt is ended, much less of the items mentioned should be fed, to allow the animals a natural period of rest.

Since breeding activity in the wild usually takes place in the rainy season, a more frequent showering by a mister or sprinkler system provides an additional stimulus.

Nest Boxes and Material   Like all parrots—with two exceptions, the Monk Parakeet *(Myiopsitta monachus)* and the Ground Parrot *(Pezoporus wallicus)*—cockatoos are cavity breeders. The white color of the eggs, the early stage of development at hatching, and the long period in the nest are adaptations to this. In the wild, a clutch will usually be found in a hollow tree trunk or branch; only small numbers of large nest holes are available. Thus nests of the Galah *(E. roseicapillus)* have been found in cavities only 18 cm. in diameter; four young birds were raised in them. These observations indicate that overly large boxes or tree trunks are not always the best nesting sites. Every cockatoo fancier who has ever dragged heavy tree trunks home from the woods would shake his head on seeing these nests.

The best opportunities for successful breeding are ensured by offering the animals several nesting possibilities. Nest boxes, homemade from thick boards, or breeding holes in tree trunks—the size depends on the species of cockatoo—should be offered. Installed at different levels and facing in different directions, the breeding pair may select the one most suitable. In an aviary, there are, of course, relatively more possibilities; for safety the nest boxes should always be hung in the shelter room. In any case, our charges should be protected from all disturbances, if possible. Cockatoos are extremely sensitive and will often react unfavorably to disturbances; they will proceed to breed only when they feel completely safe. During this time, the animals should be left to themselves as much as possible, and even cleaning should be put off for as long as possible.

If the nest boxes are homemade, the cockatoos' natural urge to gnaw during the breeding season must be considered. Only thick hardwood boards will offer the necessary resistance to the cockatoo beak; metal bands at the edges or around the entrance hole will put a stop to the destruction. Nest boxes made of boards always have the disadvantage of a less favorable microclimate, as compared to natural breeding cavities. In natural nesting holes the rotting material of the bottom is an excellent reservoir of humidity necessary for the hatching young, but board nest boxes lack this humidity-holding substrate. Even the use of damp nesting material or regular dampening of the outside of the box will only partly correct this, which happens especially when breeding in heated shelter rooms. A partially hollow tree trunk that is rotting on the inside is, therefore, better for breeding cockatoos and, in addition, is more readily accepted. If the birds can gnaw and enlarge their nesting cavity themselves, it is an excellent breeding stimulus. If necessary, the entrance hole should be nailed up with twigs and pieces of bark for this reason.

Once one nesting cavity is accepted, the others may be removed. If a nesting facility

Above: Little Corellas (*C. s. sanguinea*) like to rest during the hot midday hours. Here, near Mount Isa, Queensland, one takes advantage of the shade at the nest entrance.
Left: Breeding pair of Goffin's Cockatoos (*C. goffini*) with fledged youngster (lowest). They exhibit the threat behavior typical of all cockatoos.
Below: Little Corella (*C. s. sanguinea*) pair with young.

Hand-reared White Cockatoo (*C. alba*).

needs to be replaced, it should be the same type and put in the same place.

It is very important that the nest box can be opened without much fuss, so the clutch and young animals can be checked. Nest boxes must be protected from vermin and have to be cleaned after every breeding. Since few cockatoo species will collect nesting material, absorbent material must be put into the box. Rotting pieces of wood, which may be found in ample supply anywhere in the woods, are most suitable; the larger pieces are gnawed by the cockatoos and so broken up. Wood shavings and peat moss, on the other hand, tend to dry too rapidly and become full of dangerous fungus spores. Cockatoos will often throw dry nesting material out of the box. The eggs, which are now rolling around on the bare wood, have little chance of hatching. As additional nesting material, there should always be fresh twigs of willows, poplars, or fruit trees,

for example, which will be collected only sporadically by most species, but regularly by the Galah *(E. roseicapillus)* and the Palm Cockatoo *(P. aterrimus)*.

Breeding and Rearing With the onset of laying, the behavior of the cockatoos changes radically. The animals, which were often very noisy during courtship, now become increasingly quiet. During this time, the number of copulations increases to four to six per day. The duration of mating is noticeable, for it may last for several minutes. Comparative values for the size of the clutch, laying interval, and the duration of incubation and nestling periods may be seen in the table below.

Because of the sometimes considerable time differences at which individual eggs are laid, it is to be expected that the young birds will hatch at intervals. Accordingly, the larger cockatoo species especially will often raise only

Breeding Cycles of the Cockatoo Species

Species	Incubation by: Female (F) Male (M)	Clutch Size (number of eggs)	Egg-laying Interval (in days)	Incubation Period (in days)	Nestling Period (in days)
Palm Cockatoo	F	1	—	30	110
Black Cockatoo	F	1-2	6	28-30	90
Red-tailed Cockatoo	F	1-3	6	28	90
Glossy Cockatoo	F	1	—	29	90
Gang-gang Cockatoo	F & M	2-3	?	26-28	55
Galah	F & M	3-6	2	22-24	55
Major Mitchell's Cockatoo	F & M	3-4	2	22-24	55
Sulphur-crested Cockatoo	F & M	2-4	2-4	22-28	50-80
Lesser Sulphur-crested Cockatoo	F & M	3-5	2	22-24	50-60
Blue-eyed Cockatoo	F & M	2	?	30	120
Salmon-crested Cockatoo	F & M	2	3	30	90
White Cockatoo	F & M	2	4	28	85
Red-vented Cockatoo	F & M	2-4	2	24-28	50
Goffin's Cockatoo	F & M	2-4	2	28	70
Little Corella	F & M	2-3	2	21	45
Long-billed Corella	F & M	2-4	2	24-28	50-70
Ducorps's Cockatoo	F & M	2-4	2	28	?
Cockatiel	F & M	4-6	2	18	33

the first-hatched young. The smaller nestmates are neglected and must starve. This mechanism, useful in the wild—practically, the second youngster is only a ready replacement in case the first one is lost—may be circumvented, if necessary, by artificial feeding in captivity. For this, it is useful to know the exact hatching date. However, too frequent disturbances must be avoided. During this period, it is not necessary to offer an additional rearing food. However, many cockatoos will change their feeding habits completely at this time. Suddenly, they will eat things that they touched only rarely before; consequently, proportions must change, or the foods offered must encompass an even greater variety.

Artificial Rearing In initial breeding attempts especially it is possible that the instinctive link between mates is not fully functional yet. Eggs laid on the aviary floor, or a clutch laid by the female in the breeding hole but not incubated by the male are the consequences. In order to salvage as much as possible, one must decide between artificial incubation with an incubator and fostering. The Cockatiel *(N. hollandicus)* is particularly well suited for fostering the small cockatoo species, because the hatched young birds are fed well, at least initially, thanks to the common repertoire of behaviors. It is useful to have an incubator ready for backup. The incubation temperature this way should initially be 38 C., rising gradually to about 40 C. toward the hatching date. The relative humidity should not be less than 70–80%; it too must be increased as the hatching date approaches. Good ventilation must be ensured; the eggs are turned twice daily. A cooling of the clutch, on the other hand, must be prevented; even in the wild, the eggs are usually never unattended, because the parents take turns at incubating. The noise of a continuous ventilator, as well as drafts, may damage the developing embryos, because conditions in natural breeding cavities are always the same.

Twelve hours after hatching, artificial rearing may be begun; initially the chicks continue to feed off their store of yolk. This is not easy, especially with cockatoos, as will become clear if one knows the feeding behavior of parents and young animals in natural rearing. If both parents incubate, the newly hatched young are fed from the beginning by both parents. They enclose the beak of the young bird with their own, pulling the head and neck of the young upward slightly and executing rapid jerking movements. Accordingly, attempts at feeding present many difficulties, and the bird keeper is confronted with a true test of his patience.

Recently hatched chicks can be fed initially by means of a one-way syringe. With a rubber probe attached—this can easily be fashioned from a rubber valve—the food mush is injected directly into the crop. A proven rearing food consists of a mixture of baby cereal and dextrose, enriched with some edible calcium and drops of a multivitamin preparation. Initially, there should be five or six feedings per day, taking care not to fill the crop too full. In between, the young are put in a dark box with soft padding. To substitute for the brooding parents, sufficient heat must be provided. Many breeders prefer to feed the nestlings with their own mouthes initially. After about twenty or thirty days, the method of feeding is changed; a spoon is used to feed the begging young. Initially runny, the food mixture gradually should have a firmer consistency now; it is enriched by grated carrots, apples, and finely chopped chicken eggs. Commercially available rearing foods may be mixed in; the proportion of ground seed is slowly increased. This ensures a sufficient supply of roughage. It is wise to hold the beak of the young between thumb and index finger after each bit of food is given; up-and-down movements imitate the natural feeding movements. At fifty to sixty days, the young usually will begin to accept the food mush from a flat dish. If we now add millet kernels and finely chopped, hulled sunflower seed, the step toward complete self-sufficiency is usually not very great.

Sulphur-crested Cockatoo (*C. g. galerita*) at 4 days of age. The yellow primary down is easily seen here.

The 4-day-old chick, now placed in a larger saucer, which is used in the subsequent photographs to give a sense of scale.

At 18 days, the primary down has almost disappeared, and its eyes are beginning to open.

By 25 days, the feather shafts have already pierced the skin.

The 32-day-old chick screeches with fright when it is taken from the nest box.

The crest feathers are now visible, at 40 days of age.

Now 51 days old, the young bird is almost completely feathered and has almost attained adult weight.

Age, 69 days. This youngster left the nest when it was 82 days old.

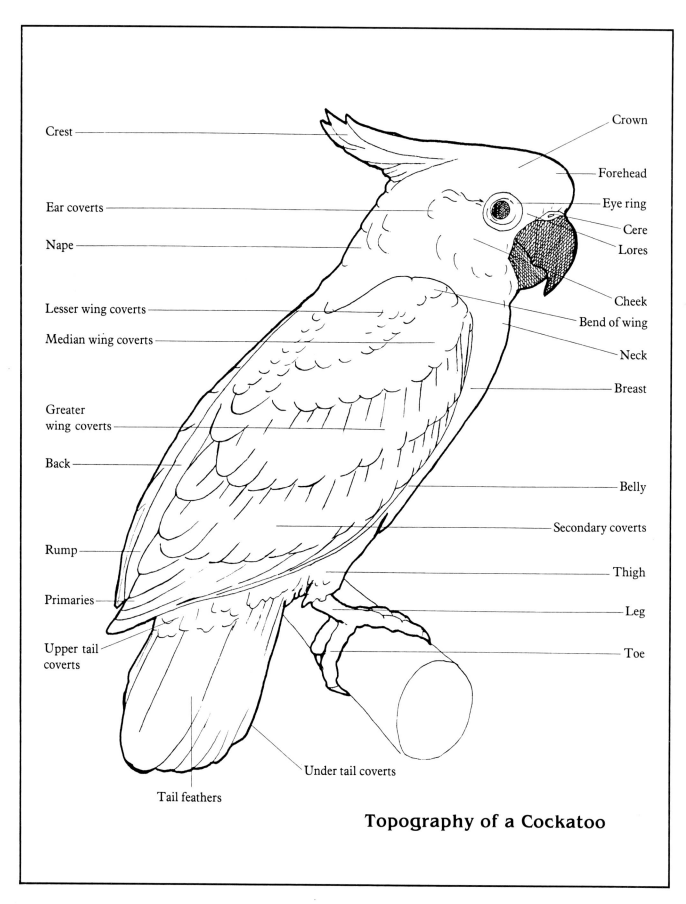

Crest

Ear coverts

Nape

Lesser wing coverts

Median wing coverts

Greater
wing coverts

Back

Rump

Primaries

Upper tail
coverts

Tail feathers

Under tail coverts

Crown

Forehead

Eye ring

Cere

Lores

Cheek

Bend of wing

Neck

Breast

Belly

Secondary coverts

Thigh

Leg

Toe

Topography of a Cockatoo

Species Accounts

Genus *PROBOSCIGER* Kuhl 1820

One species.

Palm Cockatoo
Prosciger aterrimus
(Gmelin) 1788

German: *Palmkakadu, Ararakakadu*
French: *Microglosse noir*
Dutch: *Ararakaketoe, Grote Zwart Kaketoe*

Three subspecies Forshaw describes three subspecies of this monotypic genus, which differ mainly only in body and crest size. Other authors distinguish five subspecies; in the opinion of the author, it has not been sufficiently clarified yet whether these are indeed subspecies or merely geographical races.

1. *P. aterrimus aterrimus* (Gmelin)
Characteristics: Size, about 55–60 cm. Plumage mainly gray black; wings and front black; crest formed by many narrow backward-curving crown feathers; bright red bare cheek patches extending from the base of the gray black beak to the eye; tongue red with black tip; iris dark brown; legs and feet gray. The sexes do not differ from each other in coloration, but the females are somewhat smaller and have a more delicate head and upper mandible. Young birds are recognizable by the pale yellow spots on the under wing coverts; the beak is light gray to horn-colored.
Distribution: Rainforests of the Cape York Peninsula in northern Australia and in the adja-

cent parts of New Guinea in the vicinity of the Orimo river; Aru Islands.

2. *P. a. goliath* (Kuhl)
Characteristics: Larger than nominate form: 60–70 cm.; plumage darker gray.
Distribution: Western New Guinea in the region of the Vogelkop mountains, and southern New Guinea; western Papuan Islands, Waigeo.

3. *P. a. stenolophus* (van Oort)
Characteristics: Body size and coloration like *goliath*, but with a smaller crest.
Distribution: Northern New Guinea; Yapen.

Life in the Wild Although the Palm Cockatoo is certainly the most showy cockatoo because of its considerable size, observations of this species in the wild are by no means frequent to this day. Often this elegant flyer is identified only by its flight silhouette and by its voice before it is out of sight of its observers, protected by the leafy canopy of the rainforest.

The Palm Cockatoo usually stays, singly or in pairs, in the treetops of the rainforest; occasionally it is found in small groups. Its range extends as far as the southern border of the rainforest on the Cape York Peninsula. Only rarely is it found in the surrounding savannas. Since these forest areas are more and more exploited and pushed back by commercial interests, it is vital that national parks and reservations be maintained to guarantee the survival of this impressive cockatoo species. In Australia, Palm Cockatoos are completely protected, but in the future, additional efforts must be made to preserve the habitat of these

P. a. goliath

Palm Cockatoo,
Probosciger aterrimus

animals. In Australia they are threatened mainly by the mining industry; in New Guinea, they are increasingly displaced by the steadily growing population.

Forshaw describes them as definite slugabeds among the cockatoos, becoming active only long after sunrise. Before they leave their sleeping places on the highest branches of tall trees, they preen their feathers for a while. About an hour after daybreak the cockatoos begin to call to each other, with the usual result that a troop of five or six animals gather on a tall tree. Together, they fly to search for food. Palm Cockatoos are excellent flyers which—with strongly flapping wings about 40 cm. long—can quickly move around their home range. In flight, two-syllable contact calls are uttered; the first note is soft and low, the second a shrill, high whistle. Often a short, monosyllabic whistle can be heard; the alarm call, on the other hand, is a brief, harsh shriek. In the falling

dusk, the author repeatedly heard prolonged, sad "mourning calls."

Palm Cockatoos eat mainly seeds, nuts, berries, and also fruits, but do not ignore the larvae of wood beetles, which they dig from rotting wood by means of their powerful beaks. Leaf buds and young shoots enrich their diet. Not even the hardest seed hulls can resist the mighty beak. The fruit of the *Pandanus* palm, the seed of which man can extract only with tools, is a preferred delicacy; the thick, fibrous hull is opened easily and the seed eaten. Because of the special shape of the beak, both small and large seeds can be held and hulled. Because of several grooves in the upper mandible, it can be compared to an adjustable nutcracker. Clamped in one such groove, the nut is pried open with the lower mandible, and the kernel is removed piece by piece by the extremely agile tongue. On several occasions the author was able to observe Palm Cockatoos eating small nuts and seeds. Held in portions in the lower mandible, they are individually pushed forward by the tongue and cracked. However, this mode of eating is characteristic not only of the Palm Cockatoo, but has also been observed in the Sulphur-crested Cockatoo *(C. galerita),* the White Cockatoo *(C. alba),* and in the Salmon-crested Cockatoo *(C. moluccensis).*

The intimidation behavior of this cockatoo, which can often be seen on congregating trees, is particularly impressive. Since birds of both sexes, as well as sexually immature young animals, exhibit this behavior, it should not be classed with courtship behavior, but with agonistic behavior. The displays are always accompanied by a whistling contact call of two syllables. As the first note of the call is voiced, the bird assumes an erect posture. After uttering the shrill, prolonged second note, the cockatoo lunges forward while spreading its wings. The author also considers the threat behavior of this cockatoo to be of interest. The animals bring their heads to the level of the branch on which they are perched and twist them so that the crests point downward. Growling sounds are uttered, and the strong red color of the cheek patches indicates the animals' excited state. Rhythmical stomping movements of

The tropical rainforest of the Cape York Peninsula is the home of the Palm Cockatoo (*P. a. aterrimus*) and the Sulphur-crested Cockatoo (*C. g. galerita*).

the feet also signify this excitement. The body feathers are spread to demonstrate power and strength to the opponent, "more bluff than bite."

The breeding season is closely coupled to the rainy season and lasts from August to February. It frequently happens that water enters the nest; thus collecting nesting material may be considered an adaptation. Both mates bring thin twigs in their beaks into the nest, where they are carefully splintered. The bottom of the breeding cavity is thus covered with a layer of bits of twigs, which, according to the research of Forshaw, are not only thin, but sometimes may be up to 20–30 cm. thick. Both entering rainwater and the liquid excrement of the young animals seep through this bed of twigs. Although Eastman and Hunt describe a clutch of two eggs, as a rule only one elliptical egg (averaging 49.0 × 36.5 mm.) is laid onto this substrate. If it is lost, a second egg may be laid. The female alone incubates for thirty days and is fed during this period by the male. The nestling period is often stated to be sixty days; in the opinion of the author, however, this appears too short. Breeding cavities are usually at considerable heights and, with a diameter of 25–50 cm., are often more than one meter deep. Once accepted, the same nests are used year after year.

Keeping The first Palm Cockatoos were imported already during the last century; the zoological garden in Frankfurt received a specimen in 1875; an animal that came to London in 1927 is said to be still living there in the zoo. Today, many zoological gardens keep this cockatoo; in Vogelpark Walsrode, there are several pairs of this species. Since the early 1970s, Palm Cockatoos have been imported more often once again, but always in limited numbers and consequently at high prices. While initially the animals arrived in a deplorable state and frequently died after a few weeks, the author has seen several imports in recent years that were in good condition. In most cases, these were animals that came via

Bangkok or Singapore. Since export from Australia is forbidden and smuggling such large animals is risky, most of the animals that reach us are likely to have come from New Guinea. During a visit to an exporter in Singapore, the author was able to see fourteen impeccable specimens which, according to information from the dealer, originated in West Irian.

Basically, only a large, roomy aviary of stable construction is suitable for keeping these birds. Animals which are not kept in a well-planned flight often appear bored and listless. If a Palm Cockatoo is in bad shape, this is evident from its gray pink cheek; healthy animals have salmon red facial skin, dark red when excited. Kept in a large aviary they are in constant motion and exhibit their interesting behavioral repertoire, and they will also quickly become affectionate toward their keeper.

A bird fancier of the author's acquaintance calls his Palm Cockatoos the "pacifists" of the species he keeps. No aggressive behavior toward other species kept together with them has ever been observed; however, this might change when they become inclined to breed. The author has even caught untamed Palm Cockatoos by hand, without restraining their heads. Despite the enormous, destructive-looking beaks, the animals did not bite. R. Low records similar observations; however, this must not be taken to be the rule.

Acclimation is by no means so difficult as the change in diet. Although Palm Cockatoos occasionally have been wintered in the cold, even in our latitudes, it is preferable to house them in an aviary with a heated shelter room.

Feeding It occasionally happens with these specialized feeders that newly imported animals refuse to eat at all. Here, it is the duty of the conscientious importer to get the cockatoos to accept food. Cembra and other nuts are usually taken first and should continue to be a considerable part of the diet even after acclimation. Sunflower, corn, and small seeds are also taken. Fruit and green food of all kinds should be offered. Fresh peas and the pits of apricots and peaches are welcome changes in the menu.

Breeding No further legal importation of the Palm Cockatoo can be expected after the revision of the Washington Convention [on International Trade in Endangered Species (CITES)] went into effect in June 1981. The countries of origin of this cockatoo will not issue export documents, and export papers from Singapore or Bangkok will not be recognized. Hence, this cockatoo species should be kept only for the purpose of breeding it.

Because of the size of the animals, a breeding log with an interior diameter of about 40 cm. must be offered. Since in the wild the Palm Cockatoo prefers tall nesting trees, it should be installed as high as possible. Pairing may cause difficulties because sometimes the sex of the animals cannot be clearly determined. Owning both a larger and a smaller bird does not guarantee that these are a pair; they may be animals of the same sex, though of different subspecies or geographical races. Only thorough observation of the cockatoos or endoscopic sex determination offers certainty.

Palm Cockatoos have already been bred in captivity many times. In Germany, however, there have been no proven breeding results thus far. In several instances the author unmasked so-called homebreds as fresh imports; the condition of the plumage is usually an unmistakable indicator here. When questioned, none of the "breeders" could give precise details about duration of incubation, time in the nest, or breeding behavior, so that such reports of success should be doubted; often they serve to legitimize illegally imported birds.

It appears that the first totally successful breeding occurred for Sheffler in the U.S.A. in 1944. In the London Zoo, an animal more than forty-five years old repeatedly laid infertile eggs, even though she was kept together with a cock. Forshaw reports several successful breedings in captivity; however, in these instances the young had to be reared by hand,

since they were abandoned by their parents. The reason for this faulty behavior might have been an unbalanced diet. In 1968, R. T. Lynn of Sydney, Australia, succeeded in rearing one young bird. A pair about thirty years old, which he obtained from the collection of Sir Edward Hallstrom, bred successfully for the first time.

In August 1970, three Palm Cockatoos, a male and two females, were in the Taronga Zoo in Sydney; shortly afterwards, a second cock was acquired. The animals were kept in pairs in aviaries with an area of about 18 meters square. In the spring of 1971, one pair accepted a breeding log 1.50 m. high and 0.38 m. in diameter. Both mates carried twigs about 30 cm. long into the nest, where they were broken up. Although this behavior – protecting the nestling or the clutch from rainwater – loses its original significance in captivity, a breeding pair should still have a sufficient supply of twigs available. Constructing a nest is innate and therefore an indispensible part of breeding behavior. On the nesting substrate thus constructed, a single egg was laid; on November 30 of the same year, the soft cheeping of the young bird could be heard for the first time. The incubation period is given as 31–35 days. Initially the youngster developed nicely. It was fed by the hen only; the cock was never seen in the breeding cavity, but he fed the female regularly. In January 1972, the male fell ill with a supposed *Candida* infection, and since transmission of the fungus to the female and the chick was feared, the youngster was taken from the nest for treatment and reared by hand.

Naked at hatching, the young Palm Cockatoo was covered with gray down at the age of two weeks; between the fifth and sixth week, the body was covered with developing feathers. When the nestling was taken from the breeding log at the age of about sixty days, it was almost completely feathered. After another twenty-five days, feather growth appeared to be complete. However, it still could be clearly recognized as a young bird by pale yellow spots, particularly on the nape and throat. At the end of March the animal suddenly became ill, and it died on April 3; a postmortem showed that a psittacosis infection was the cause of death. A short time afterward, the breeding cock died of the same infection.

The second pair bred for the first time in May 1973, producing one youngster. In a tree trunk more than 2.0 m. long (0.78 m. in diameter), infertile eggs had been laid repeatedly during the preceding years. The youngster developed without any problems and left the nest after 100 to 110 days. Two weeks later, it was still flying clumsily, and after six weeks it was still being fed by its parents.

At the Leipzig Zoo, the first young Palm Cockatoo was reared in 1981; at present their breeding pair is successfully rearing a youngster for the third time.

Genus *CALYPTORHYNCHUS* Desmarest 1826 — black cockatoos

Three species   All three species inhabit Australia, Tasmania, and some nearby islands. They show more or less pronounced sexual dimorphism. Only the females incubate, but both sexes care for the young.

Black Cockatoo *Calyptorhynchus funereus* (Shaw) 1794

German: *Brauner Rabenkakadu*
French: *Cacatoès funèbre*
Dutch: *Bruine kakatoe*

C. f. funereus, female

Black Cockatoo, *Calyptorhynchus funereus*

Intimidation posture of the Black Cockatoo (*C. f. baudinii*). The dark beak and uniformly white tail band indicate that this is a male.

Four subspecies Four subspecies with partially separate ranges can be distinguished. In addition, differences in plumage coloration and courtship behavior separate the populations.

1. *C. funereus funereus* (Shaw)
Characteristics: Size, about 65 cm.
Male: Plumage mainly brownish black; breast, belly, head, and neck feathers edged in yellow; ear region yellow; central tail feathers brownish black, yellow band of the outer tail feathers spotted with brownish black; beak dark gray; iris dark brown; legs and feet brownish gray. Female: Brighter yellow in the ear region; tail band more markedly spotted with brownish black; beak horn-colored. Young birds resemble the adult females; young males have paler ear spots.
Distribution: Southeastern Australia from central Queensland through eastern New South Wales to Victoria.

2. *C. f. xanthanotus* Gould
Characteristics: Like the nominate form, but smaller and with a shorter tail.
Distribution: Tasmania and some larger islands of the Bass Straits.

3. *C. f. baudinii* Lear
Characteristics: Size, about 58 cm. Male: Plumage mainly pale brown black; ear region and feather edges murky white; tail bands white with faint brown black spotting. Female: As in the nominate form, recognizable by more intense markings.
Distribution: Extreme southwestern Australia.

4. *C. f. latirostris* Carnaby
Characteristics: Like *baudinii*, but with a broader, shorter beak.
Distribution: Dry interior districts of southwestern Australia.

Black Cockatoo (*C. f. baudinii*), female.

Life in the Wild Within their range, Black Cockatoos used to be an everyday sight, but they are far more rare today. *C. f. baudinii* especially is endangered and is strictly protected in Australia. Field research done between 1970 and 1974 in the vicinity of Perth indicated a pronounced decrease in breeding pairs. According to this study, only every third pair successfully raised one youngster per year. The reasons for this are the increasing land cultivation, with the concomitant disappearance of habitat, nesting sites, and food. A second study, in which seventy-five breeding pairs were observed over several years, showed more encouraging results: In three years, two young per pair were reared. Breeding behavior and success seem to depend very much on climatic factors and food availability. If sufficient food is available, during incubation the female will be provisioned by the male almost exclusively. In arid areas, however, it was observed that females periodically leave the nest even during incubation in order to search for food. Depending on the conditions, at fledging the young weigh 83–97% of the adult weight. Since Black Cockatoos are extremely long-lived animals, declining breeding productivity is not immediately as apparent as a decrease in population density. Protective measures that will above all guarantee breeding success of the remaining pairs are necessary.

Black Cockatoos inhabit dense forests, but occasionally they can be found in dry scrubland. According to habitat, several geographical races are distinguished; two separate populations in southwestern Australia also show morphological differences in the shape of the mandibles as well as in size and therefore are listed as separate subspecies. The Black Cockatoo is a loud, conspicuous bird that usually can be observed in pairs or groups of three. Even when attacking *Pinus* plantations or newly cleared fields in small flocks, these groups of three stick closely together; they are certainly breeding pairs with one youngster. Larger flocks, which may include more than a thou-

sand animals, are observed only outside the breeding season.

Their main diet consists of *Eucalyptus* and *Banksia* seeds, but the seeds of *Acacia* and other native and introduced trees and bushes are also popular. Although their food is found to a greater extent in trees, they will come to the ground to eat fallen fruit and to drink. At such times they are extremely cautious, and it is very difficult to approach them. While the animals are eating, one or two birds remain as lookouts in nearby trees and give the alarm signal if danger is near. The group flees immediately; their flight is slow and unusually buoyant and elegant for their body size. Contact calls, disyllabic and drawn out, are uttered. Besides vegetable food, the larvae of wood-boring insects are probably their main staple. Even more eagerly than other species of black cockatoos they search the bark and wood of the trees for insect larvae, which they will pick from rotting wood daintily with the beak. In this way, they destroy a lot of damaging insects; torn strips of bark and fiber are clear signs of cockatoos searching for food. The damage to plantations, particularly in southwestern Australia, leads to merciless persecution by the farmers, despite protective measures.

Many studies and observations indicate that the Black Cockatoo undertakes regular, seasonal migrations. Several observations show that the birds from the interior wander to the southern and western coasts during summer. Thus, large gatherings were observed in extreme southwestern Australia from March to April on several occasions; weeks later, the animals suddenly disappeared again. It is assumed that they returned to the wheat zones in the interior, where large numbers were sighted from April to October.

In southern Queensland and northern New South Wales, breeding takes place between March and August, while in southeastern Australia, it occurs from July to January. In Tasmania nests with eggs and young were found even in February. In southwestern

Australia, the breeding season lasts from August to November.

Weeks before the first egg is laid, mates begin preparing the roomy breeding cavity. Tall trees, usually some kind of *Eucalyptus,* are the preferred nest sites. The animals in turn will spend about ten minutes enlarging the nest hole by eager gnawing; in between, they fly from branch to branch around the area. Especially during this time, courtship feeding as an element of pair bonding may be observed frequently. The display of the male is simple, yet at the same time impressive. The crest is raised and the fanned tail is presented to the female; the tail band has a definite signalling function.

One or two eggs (averaging 48.5 × 35.0 mm.) are laid with an interval of five to seven days. The female incubates the clutch alone from the first day on and is fed regularly by the male. The latter approaches the nest with extreme caution and signals his arrival to the female by soft contact calls from far away. In the immediate vicinity of the breeding cavity, however, he becomes absolutely quiet; thus the nesting place will remain hidden from possible enemies in the area. Feeding takes place, as a rule, on a branch outside the nest. The incubation period lasts for twenty-nine days; once the first chick has hatched, it and the female depend entirely on care by the male during the first few days. Initially, the cock provides both with food; only after about two weeks will the female also leave the nest to search for food. A second youngster, hatched after an interval of five days, is neglected and dies; it is merely a kind of natural reserve in case the first nestling is lost. After some weeks, the nestling is fed by both parents only in the early morning and evening. About three months after hatching, the flighted young bird leaves the nest, but it will be provided with food for another four months. In the second year, the beak of the young bird becomes dark, and in the fourth year it will itself be ready to breed.

Keeping   Like all the *Calyptorhynchus* species,

Black Cockatoos are rare in captivity. In accordance with export restrictions, their export from Australia is forbidden; only a few zoological gardens outside that continent exhibit them. Even in former years, the animals came in only seldom and in small numbers. The pairs occasionally offered during 1980–81 were all birds that had been smuggled from their home ranges and found their way to us via Bangkok or Singapore. In 1981, the author was offered a pair of Yellow-tailed Black Cockatoos by a dealer from Thailand at a horrendous price. Since young animals are usually imported – they acclimate more easily – and their sex cannot yet be determined, such an investment should be considered doubly carefully. Fortunately, the high price will scare off private collectors, so that usually only fanciers with serious breeding intentions will decide to buy.

In acclimation, adapting to our climate causes fewer difficulties than the change of dietary habits. A Belgian bird fancier could keep his animals from sure death after a one-week hunger strike only by offering them rotted branches studded with wood grubs. Freshly collected pine cones and mealworms are important staple foods during acclimation. Once acclimated, these cockatoos are quite robust and not very sensitive to low temperatures. Housing them in a roomy outdoor aviary with a shelter room goes without saying.

Feeding   Sunflower seed, teazle, and various small seeds, as well as all kinds of nuts and berries and different kinds of fruits should be offered, though they often are not taken at all. Fresh branches for gnawing and branches infested with insects should not be lacking; as a substitute, mealworms may be offered. Finely ground beef heart, with breadcrumbs added to make a crumby mass and mixed into the seed mixture, is enjoyed by many cockatoos and should be given to this species especially.

Breeding   Although Black Cockatoos are kept somewhat more widely than other members of the genus, reports of successful breeding are almost never to be found. Kept in spacious aviaries, the birds generally stay in good condition. Nest boxes, fastened as high as possible in the outdoor flight, are very readily accepted. In the Adelaide Zoo several eggs have been laid; most often there was no incubation, or the hatched young were not reared. The unbalanced diet must be blamed. Only when it is possible to find a substitute for the insect larvae that are the primary food in the wild can breeding success be expected. Finely ground meat, perhaps mixed with cooked millet, or cooked and raw bones might be tried.

At the Westbury Zoo in Tasmania, youngsters of the nominate form were reared in both 1967 and 1968. An Australian bird fancier is said to have succeeeded in 1971. In 1976, in the laboratories of the CSIRO Division of Wildlife Research near Perth, a youngster of the subspecies *C. f. baudinii* fledged.

Red-tailed Cockatoo
Calyptorhynchus magnificus
(Shaw) 1790

German: *Banks-Rabenkakadu, Rotschwanzkakadu*
French: *Cacatoès de Banks*
Dutch: *Banks Zwarte Roodstaart-Kaketoe*

Four subspecies   Altogether four subspecies have been described and named; their ranges overlap, at least in part. Intergradation in the areas of overlap is possible, since they are not yet genetically separate. Since specimens of the various subspecies differ mainly in size and such a character alone does not suffice for systematic separation, taxonomy of this kind seems unsatisfactory to the author. The different subspecies may merely be geographical races of one species; the absence of geographical barriers, at least partially, in the area of distribution of the various groups seems to suggest this.

C. m. magnificus, female

Red-tailed Cockatoo,
Calyptorhynchus magnificus

Near watercourses, the eucalyptus savannah gradually becomes a gallery forest with dense underbrush, as here along the East Alligator River in Arnhem Land in northern Australia. Little Corellas (*C. s. sanguinea*), Sulphur-crested (*C. g. galerita*), and Red-tailed (*C. m. macrorhynchus*) cockatoos are found here.

1. *C. magnificus magnificus* (Shaw)

Characteristics: Size, about 62 cm. Male: Basic coloration black; back, nape, and breast washed with brown; central tail feathers black, the others have a wide red band in the middle; beak dark gray; iris dark brown; legs gray brown. Female: Plumage mainly brownish black with numerous yellow spots on head, neck, median wing coverts, and wing flights; feathers of the lower belly edged with pale yellow; tail band orange with black barring; beak horn-colored. The young resemble the adult female; young males take four years to attain full coloration. After the first molt, the yellow markings on the head and wing coverts diminish, breast barring lessens, and the tail band loses more of its barred pattern; in the third year, barring is almost completely gone, as is the spotting. The beak becomes darker, and in the fourth year the animals molt into adult plumage.

Distribution: Eastern Australia from the Cape York Peninsula to southern New South Wales, as well as in adjacent areas of South Australia and Victoria.

95

2. *C. m. macrorhynchus* Gould

Characteristics: Adult males similar in size and coloration to the nominate form; tail band of the female slightly yellow with little orange and weaker barring; heavier beak.

Distribution: Northern Australia: from the Kimberly District, West Australia, along the coast to the Gulf of Carpentaria.

3. *C. m. samueli* Mathews

Characteristics: Smaller than the nominate form; size, about 52 cm.; tail band of the female marked with orange.

Distribution: Central Australia, including southwestern Queensland and New South Wales.

4. *C. m. naso* Gould

Characteristics: Size, about 55 cm.; crest shorter and more rounded.

Distribution: Southwestern Australia.

Life in the Wild As Red-tailed Cockatoos are essentially nomadic, their presence in a given area depends on the availability of food, as a rule. They are—as can be seen from the morphology of the beak—mainly seed and nut eaters, so that their appearance in the area is closely timed to the ripening of the seeds. This species may be observed in the most different habitats; open forests near rivers and waterholes are their preferred resting places, but they are also found in grasslands. Formerly an everyday occurrence in their range, they have become much rarer in most places and are therefore fully protected in all the Australian states.

They are usually sighted in pairs, family groups, or small flocks, but often large flocks of up to one hundred animals will assemble. In September 1980, A. Fergenbauer was able to observe such a flock near Darwin. Red-tailed Cockatoos are noisy and for this reason conspicuous. They shriek almost without pause. In flight, they utter a rolling, metallic-sounding contact call. Although they spend the greater part of the day in tall trees feeding, they do come to the ground to look for fallen fruit and seeds. Their clumsy, waddling walk is striking; in branches, however, they are skillful climbers. Their flight is buoyant, and it is not uncommon to see them flying on moonlit nights.

Red-tailed Cockatoos have seldom been observed collecting and eating the larvae of wood beetles and moths from the branches of the trees and bushes. They feed mainly on seed and nuts, especially those of *Eucalyptus, Acacia, Casuarina,* and *Banksia.* When they crack the seed capsules with their strong beaks, it can be heard for quite a distance. Although they are less cautious while eating, it is seldom possible to approach them without having the group fly away, shrieking loudly, warned by the alarm call of one of their number. Blossoms and fruits are also eaten gladly; often the cockatoos will bite off entire twigs, which are then held in the foot and harvested with the beak.

In such a large range, the breeding season varies. Red-tailed Cockatoos breed between May and September throughout most of their range, but Forshaw mentions the months October through April as the breeding season in western Victoria and southeastern South Australia.

Weeks before laying, courting by the male may be observed. Initially he perches in a normal sitting position on a branch. The body plumage is smoothed down, the crest raised. Cheek and frontal feathers are raised, so that the beak is partially hidden. The bends of the wings are lifted, and the tail only partly fanned. Rhythmic courtship calls may be heard. Four to five low calls are followed by a short pause. After four to six such bouts of calling, the male suddenly assumes a sharply upright position by locking the intertarsal joints. A forward bow follows, with the tail spread wide and bent upward so that the red band in the fanned tail dazzles. The body sinks back to the branch, and the fanned tail is closed. Another jerky bow follows, again accompanied with fanning and bending the tail upward. As courting intensifies, the cockatoo bends even farther forward, extends his wings completely, and holds the fanned tail straight up. He remains in this position for two to three seconds with trembling wings; then the display is abruptly terminated. This courtship display is interrupted by choking movements of the head, and mate feeding follows.

For its nest the Red-tailed Cockatoo chooses a hollow branch or hole in the trunk of a tree that usually stands in a clearing or grows beside a river. Usually these breeding cavities are situated very high up and are consequently hard for humans to reach. One or two eggs (averaging 51.0 × 35.5 mm.) are laid at an interval of five to seven days and are incubated by the female only. After an incubation period of about thirty days—during this time the male feeds the female several times a day outside the nest—the young hatch. During a nestling period of about three months, one chick is reared by both parents. Even after fledging, it depends on the care of its parents for about four months until it will eat by itself. According to reports by Prof. Immelmann, the youngster of the previous year is said to remain with the parents and to participate actively in rearing its younger sibling.

Keeping The nominate form is the most common in captivity. Birds of this species reached us already in the previous century and could be admired in the London Zoo in 1862 and in Berlin in 1879. In Europe they are still rare nowadays, and only a few zoos have been able to acquire some of these animals by exchange. The San Diego Zoo received some animals in 1950 from Sir Edward Hallstrom; they could be exported from their homeland only for the purpose of aviary breeding.

These impressive birds thrive only in roomy flights; in cages or small aviaries, they appear lazy. Anyone who has ever seen the splendid flight style of these cockatoos will reject such accommodations. The Duke of Bedford kept Red-tailed Cockatoos at liberty; according to his reports, they are not sensitive to cold but tend to catch colds in fog and snow. A. Preussiger of Neuwied for several years wintered his animals

in an outdoor aviary with an attached, unheated shelter, without their being adversely affected. Hand-reared males especially may be very affectionate and may even learn to say a few words; young females, on the other hand, usually lose their tameness quite quickly once they are paired. The Duke of Bedford describes his hand-reared Red-tailed Cockatoos as the most lovable parrots he ever had in his collection. Once acclimated, Red-tailed Cockatoos are very long-lived animals; documentation shows that one specimen in the London Zoo lived for more than forty years. It is difficult to accustom fresh imports to new food, but this is not as great a problem as with other members of this genus.

Feeding Sunflower seed, hemp, canary, and millet; all kinds of nuts and berries, corn (cooked or soaked), half-ripe oats or wheat are offered, and the birds should always have a wide selection of fruits and green food at their disposal. Conifer seeds are ignored in the wild as well as in captivity. They usually reject mealworms offered as a substitute for the animal foods occasionally taken in the wild; feeding cheese, bones, or ground meat should be attempted. Farmer's cheese or yogurt, mixed with fruit, is usually accepted.

Breeding The Red-tailed Cockatoo is the black cockatoo most often bred in captivity, but with this species too captive propagation is not unproblematical. As a consequence of being housed in small aviaries that hardly take into account the animals' need for movement, clutches are often infertile. Thus the pair kept for several years by A. Preussiger of Neuwied laid two eggs each spring, which were not incubated, however, and were not fertile.

Breeding first succeeded for the Duke of Bedford in 1939 in England. In December, the female laid a single egg on the floor of the shelter room. Because of the cold weather, the youngster was taken in after hatching and reared by hand. Hallstrom in Sydney, who kept several pairs, bred them for the first time in Australia in 1943; in the following years, several successful breedings followed.

At the Adelaide Zoo young were reared several times; the first reports of success came from the year 1945; one youngster was produced. The female laid two eggs, of which only one was fertile. After a nestling period of ninety-six days, the youngster left the nest. The male of the breeding pair was documented at thirty-six years of age at this time; it had been in the collection of the zoo since 1913. The female of a second pair laid a single egg on the floor of the flight and incubated it successfully. The young bird left the "nest" after seventy-five days and, as in the previous instance, was fed by its parents for another four months.

Since 1961, the Adelaide Zoo has reported breeding successes almost regularly. The keeper, F. Bohner, described a successful breeding of the subspecies *C. m. naso* in 1976.

Female Red-tailed Cockatoo (*C. m. macrorhynchus*) eating eucalyptus seeds; photographed in northern Australia in the vicinity of Darwin.

Red-tailed Cockatoo (*C. m. magnificus*), male.

Early in 1975, the pair accepted a nesting log 1.75 m. high, with an interior diameter of 30 cm. In March of that year, the female entered the breeding cavity for the first time, and the first egg was laid on April 22. It was not incubated, and artificial incubation showed that it was infertile. A second egg, laid twenty-eight days later, was also infertile. In 1976, the first egg was laid on February 13 and incubated for twenty-eight days. A nest inspection revealed a three-day-old chick with yellow down. On the tenth day, the skin became darker because of the developing feather shafts; at that time, the eyes were still half closed. At the age of nine weeks, the youngster was already being fed and preened at the nest entrance. At the age of three months, the little cockatoo left the nesting log. At the age of twelve months, it was still being fed occasionally by the female. The keeper separated it from its parents only when another youngster fledged in 1977. In the following years, the pair was again successful. With admirable regularity, one youngster per year was reared. Sex could be determined when it left the nesting log: the plumage of young males is darker, and their spots are less pronounced. In addition, they usually are louder and more ostentatious in their behavior right from the beginning.

In the middle of the 1970s, a pair at Auckland Zoo, New Zealand, also bred successfully several times. The first successful breeding in the U.S.A. was reported by the San Diego Zoo in 1954. In 1950, the zoo received some young birds that had been bred by Hallstrom; between 1955 and 1970, as many as fifteen young Red-tailed Cockatoos were reared by hand.

These successes show that more Australian bird fanciers than do at present should devote themselves to the breeding of this impressive cockatoo. Because of extensive clearing of forests to gain land and because intensive hunting continues, its numbers continue to decline. Zoos as well as private bird fanciers should be ready to undertake cooperative breeding programs.

Glossy Cockatoo
Calyptorhynchus lathami
(Temminck) 1807

German: *Braunkopfkakadu*
French: *Cacatoès à tête brune*
Dutch: *Lathams Zwarte Kaketoe*

Characteristics: External appearance indicates the close relationship of this species to the Red-tailed Cockatoo. Thus it is difficult to distinguish the Glossy Cockatoo from the Red-tailed Cockatoo in the wild; they both occur in the same areas. In addition to smaller body size, the coloration of the female is the most important distinguishing characteristic. Male: Size, about 48 cm.; head, throat, nape, and belly dark brown, shading to black on the under wing coverts; back, wings, and tail black with a brownish green sheen; outer tail feathers have a

C. lathami, male

Glossy Cockatoo,
Calyptorhynchus lathami

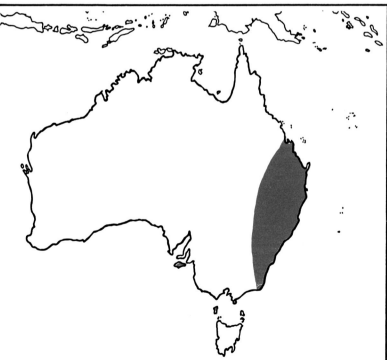

bright red band; crest shorter than in the previously described species; legs and feet gray. Female: Smaller and more brownish; yellow feathers on the side of the head and on the rump, instead of the numerous yellow spots of the Red-tailed Cockatoo female; tail band washed with yellow and broken by black barring.

Distribution: Eastern Australia from central Queensland to eastern Victoria. A confined population of less than a hundred animals lives on Kangaroo Island off South Australia. Presumably the range of this species extended to the southern coast at one time, and the island group is a relict population.

Life in the Wild Because of the predilection of Glossy Cockatoos for *Casuarina* seeds, their presence is closely linked with the occurrence of these trees. Usually the birds are observed in pairs, in family groups, or in small flocks; they prefer hilly areas and mountainous regions to open woodland. Only rarely do they congregate in larger flocks, which formerly gave the impression that these birds were very rare. Intensive field observations show, however, that this species occurs in considerably larger numbers than was supposed. The fact that the Glossy Cockatoo is arboreal and comes to the ground only for drinking makes detection more difficult. Once it has been sighted, it can be approached without special caution. Particularly when feeding, the birds are not shy, compared to other black cockatoo species, and are hardly disturbed even by an observer standing directly under the tree.

These cockatoos spend the greater part of the day in the branches feeding; their presence is betrayed by the constant clicking of their beaks. The ground beneath feeding trees is soon covered with seed hulls, twigs, and leaves. In their search for the larvae of various species of wood beetles in the trees, their strong beaks tear entire pieces of bark and splinters of wood from the trunks, which are carelessly dropped to the ground. Although the animals will also eat the seeds of *Acacia, Banksia,* and *Eucalyp-*

tus, Casuarina seeds are the main part of their diet. The woody cones are bitten off and brought to the beak with the foot. While the fruit is turned with the foot, they use considerable force to crack the hull in order to eat the oily seeds. To reach the underlayers, the cone is entirely torn apart. Once enough kernels are stored in the crop, they are said to be brought up again and broken up in the beak. "Rumination" of this kind has also been observed in other parrot species. During the dissection of a dead nestling, a kind of storage pouch was found in addition to the crop, a parchment-like sac with rudimentary muscles and two hinged valves—which tends to confirm and explain the feeding habits observed.

Glossy Cockatoos fly far in their search for food; during the extraordinarily buoyant flight, they make prolonged, soft calls. If feeding trees are close together, only local movements will be observed. Wherever the stands of *Casuarina* diminish, the cockatoos also vanish, since food suitable for rearing young is lacking. Preservation of the tree species mentioned is therefore essential for the perpetuation of this species of cockatoo, which is strictly protected under the law.

The breeding season falls between March and August; most eggs were found between April and June. Almost nothing is known about the courtship of these animals. Nest holes in hollow trunks or branches are preferred, provided they stand in clearings and the entrance is situated very high above the ground. The single egg (averaging 44.5 × 34.0 mm.—sometimes, two are laid) is incubated by the female only, as in all species of this genus. According to observations in captivity, the incubation period lasts twenty-nine days; during this time, the female is fed by the male in the morning and evening outside of the breeding cavity, in the immediate vicinity. The males are said to sleep at night away from the nest. In a clutch of two, only one youngster is reared, as a rule; during the first weeks, the female broods and protects it, but from the beginning it is fed by both parents. Since food trees are often very far from the nest, the male is usually busy seeking food all day long, so that feeding takes place only late in the evening and early in the morning. Once the young bird is about a week old, the adults are often away all day; presumably, this is possible only because the rearing food is very nutritious; in addition, the digestive system of these cockatoos works very slowly. Nothing is known about the nestling period itself; there are observations only in captivity.

Keeping Being particularly specialized feeders, these cockatoos are seldom kept in captivity. Hagenbeck received one animal as early as 1878, but it could be kept alive only for a short time. The main problem is finding an adequate substitute for the *Casuarina* seeds. Since the animals die shortly after capture, or during transport or acclimation at the latest, they are virtually never available. Keeping them anywhere but in Australia should therefore be forgone as a matter of principle because these birds are surely sentenced to death, sooner or later. It seems difficult enough to keep adult animals alive on the unfamiliar diet; breeding, which might justify keeping them, is practically impossible in the circumstances.

The only reports of successful maintenance over the years come from Australia. Sir Edward Hallstrom succeeded in the Taronga Zoo in Sydney. At times several pairs of this species were kept in the aviaries; to feed them, a man had to drive into the field daily to collect the *Casuarina* cones necessary. If the seeds were given separately or if a substitute was fed, abnormal beak growth occurred in a very short time. From insufficient use the lower mandible forked and the upper mandible grew too long a point.

Feeding Since feeding this species appropriately is hardly possible outside Australia, what follows is merely an attempt to put together an appropriate substitute. All oil-containing seeds, such as sunflower, hemp, and canary, are pertinent. According to Hallstrom, peanut butter and peanut oil must be given,

mixed into the food. Fresh twigs and conifer cones should never be omitted. Certainly, feeding these cockatoos requires the experience and courage to experiment.

Breeding In 1954 Hallstrom succeeded in rearing a youngster for the first time. Before this, long years of experimenting passed without the animals becoming interested in breeding. Two eggs were laid in a roomy log, and after an incubation period of twenty-nine days, one youngster hatched and was reared by the female alone. The male had been isolated previously, since he appeared to be completely exhausted from feeding the female during the incubation period. The young animal left the nest at thirteen weeks; there are no data about the time it took to become self-sufficient. During the 1970s, several successful breedings took place at the Taronga Zoo.

Genus *CALLOCEPHALON* Lesson 1837

One species.

Gang-gang Cockatoo *Callocephalon fimbriatum* (Grant) 1803

German: *Helmkakadu, Rotkopfkakadu*
French: *Cacatoès Gang-Gang*
Dutch: *Helmkaketoe*

Characteristics: This monotypic genus is recognizable by its forward-curving crest of plumulaceous feathers. Sexual dimorphism in this species is pronounced. Male: Size, about 35 cm.; plumage mainly gray, with the feathers edged in pale gray white, making the plumage look scaly overall; edges of the secondaries,

C. *fimbriatum*, pair

Gang-gang Cockatoo
Callocephalon fimbriatum

wing coverts, and the feathers in the area of the lower breast and belly washed with a definite pale green sheen; head, crest, and sides of the face bright red, which pales to orange red in the breast region; compact, strongly curved beak dark gray at the base, then horn-colored; legs gray. Female: Head and crest gray, feathers on breast and belly edged in orange red; tail feathers barred with gray white; beak uniformly horn-colored. Young birds resemble the female, but are recognizable by the gray white barring on the underside of the wings; young males soon show red feathers on the front and crest. *Distribution:* Coastal regions of southeastern Australia from eastern New South Wales and south Victoria to the extreme southeast of South Australia; occasionally wanders to King Island and Tasmania.

Life in the Wild The habitat of these cockatoos is mostly inaccessible montane forests

where they can be observed to altitudes of 2200 m. During the winter they move to the lower valleys and coastal areas. However, some remain in the mountains even during winter, and small groups of nonbreeding young animals are sometimes found in the low plains throughout the summer. Gang-gang Cockatoos are not very shy and have repeatedly been seen in the gardens and parks of Canberra. As a rule they appear in pairs or family groups, but flocks of fifty or more animals are no rarity. In the heart of their range, they are an everyday occurrence, so their status apparently is not threatened at present. The extensive inaccessible mountain regions are a safe refuge during the breeding season. However, in the face of the continual expansion of cultivation, it is wise that full protection is already given the Gang-gang Cockatoo.

Even today, the montane forests offer an almost inexhaustible reservoir of food for this cockatoo species. As a rule, they are observed

Gang-gang Cockatoo *(C. fimbriatum)*, male.

feeding in the tops of tall *Eucalyptus* trees. According to Dr. Kolar, they prefer the seeds of the peppermint eucalyptus, as well as *Acacia* and *Pinus*. Berries, especially those of whitethorn, and fruits, nuts, and insects and their larvae are also enjoyed. They forage very methodically and visit the same food tree for several days in order to harvest it completely; their skillful use of the foot is remarkable. While feeding, the birds emit peculiar grating calls that are more evocative of a poorly oiled door than of a cockatoo; this call is also given during flight. Gang-gang Cockatoos are extremely skillful flyers, as is suggested by their long wings; nevertheless they rarely seek safety in flight when humans approach, but at most climb to a higher branch and continue feeding there. Often they can be approached so closely that they can almost be touched. Young birds are easily captured by means of a noose put around their heads. After completing their meal, the birds sit in the highest treetops and engage in mutual preening. Often this activity is broken off, and the animals fly up, describe a few wide circles, and return to the same place. They do not stay in one place very long, but usually move on after a few days, always seeking their favorite seeds.

The breeding season falls between October and January. The optimal nesting cavities are holes in living *Eucalyptus* trees near water. The nests are situated at great heights, and the cavity is enlarged by both of the pair. Two or three eggs (averaging 36.8 × 27.5 mm.) are laid on the floor, which has been covered with wood shavings, and are incubated by both parents in turn. During the thirty-day incubation period, the clutch is left for about an hour in the early morning and evening; the pair fly out together to search for food. The young leave the nest about seven weeks after hatching and are on their own at about twelve weeks of age. However, they often remain with the adults for an extended time. Already during their first year young males can be recognized by a few red feathers on the head.

Keeping Gang-gang Cockatoos are occasionally—if always at a very high price—offered in the trade. During the 1970s, the author saw several fresh imports, with commendably quiet demeanor. Because of the revision of the Washington Convention (CITES), in the future importation will be more difficult, if not impossible, so that it must be an absolute goal to get the animals already here to breed. Although these small cockatoos are very quickly tamed and rather easily taught to speak, they are totally unsuited to being kept in a cage. Gang-gang Cockatoos absolutely require a large flight with adjoining shelter room. Their natural range indicates that these animals are not particularly sensitive to cold.

More than the other species of cockatoos, the Gang-gang Cockatoo tends to feather plucking. The females particularly exhibit this bad habit, which is almost impossible to cure once they become used to it. Several German and Swiss bird fanciers own such pitiful creatures, which of course are hardly suitable for breeding. In order to prevent boredom, wide variety both in aviary decor and in diet must be provided. Constantly available fresh twigs for gnawing may be of some help.

Feeding Since in the wild these animals live mostly on small seeds, they spend the great part of the day searching for food. If the table in their aviary is richly set, little time for eating is needed. The result is boredom, which is expressed by feather plucking. Therefore, a basic diet of only mixed millets, enriched with teazle and only a few sunflower seeds, should be offered. In this way, the animals are kept busy longer, and because of the lower fat content, they will also eat more frequently. Berries and fruit of all kinds should also be given. Since in the wild the birds also like to search the cones of different species of pines for seeds, half-ripe and ripe cones of native evergreens must also be on the menu of the Gang-gang Cockatoo. Their value lies less in nutrition than in the fact that the animals will be kept busy for hours.

Even a strong cockatoo beak finds it comparatively difficult to get to the small seeds; the animals' natural need for occupation is thus met. In order to meet the requirements for animal protein, air-dried bones may be offered, and are accepted gladly, as the author has observed.

Breeding The Gang-gang Cockatoo has been bred repeatedly in captivity. Breeding first succeeded for Mme. Lécallier in France in 1921. The pair laid two eggs in a 20-liter wine cask, which was placed high underneath the aviary roof. Both young hatched, but one died on the second day. The surviving youngster left the nest after about eight weeks and could be seen to be a cock because of some red feathers on its head. In the following years, many times two young each time were reared.

The first successful breeding in England was for the Duke of Bedford in 1938. His pair incubated in a rotten tree trunk that stood in an outdoor aviary, protected from the rain by a solid roof. From the two eggs laid in May, both young hatched after an incubation period of twenty-nine days and left the breeding cavity after a nestling period of two months.

In 1945, the first breeding successes were reported from Australia. A bird fancier living in the mountains had put a female Gang-gang Cockatoo with an injured wing into the same aviary with a Galah (E. roseicapillus). The pair bred successfully and reared two young, which were set free. This crossbreeding sheds some light on the close relationship of the two cockatoo species, which thus far had only been assumed. In the same year, breeding was also reported by Mrs. Marrifeld in Australia, and a few years later Hallstrom was successful.

The Gang-gang Cockatoo was bred for the first time in the U.S.A. in 1973 by Mrs. Velma Hart of California; a young male was reared by hand. In the next year, the birds came into the possession of Dr. J. M. Dolan, who was successful several times during the next years. He reports an incubation period of twenty-five to twenty-seven days; the nestlings open their eyes after twelve days and leave the nest at about fifty-five days. The San Diego Zoo has also successfully bred this species.

Breeding in Germany was first reported by G. Volkemer of Oberursel, who imported three pairs, which were in very poor plumage condition, from England in 1974. In the spring of 1975, one pair were once again in perfect plumage and copulated frequently. A nesting hole of pine in the shelter room was accepted; the bedding of peat and rotten wood was thrown out. The grassy sods that were put into the nest afterwards were left there. Two eggs, laid in early June, proved to be infertile. In the following year, one young bird was reared, but unfortunately it was killed in an accident. Since then, these beautiful cockatoos have been bred repeatedly by a breeder in England. As food for rearing the young, in addition to sprouted sunflower seed, bread soaked in milk, bread with honey, and bananas and apples were given. In Australia, it is said, even cooked, greasy mutton was accepted while rearing young.

Genus *EOLOPHUS* Bonaparte 1854

One species.

Galah *Eolophus roseicapillus* (Vieillot) 1817

German: *Rosakakadu*
French: *Cacatoès rosalbin*
Dutch: *Rosé Kaketoe*

Forshaw believes that this monotypic genus is transitional between the Gang-gang Cockatoo (*Callocephalon*) and the *Cacatua* cockatoos. Besides anatomical similarities and the same flight style, similarities in behavior traits support this thesis above all. In addition, the

Galah is the only species which has hybridized with the Gang-gang Cockatoo.

Two subspecies Forshaw describes two subspecies, differing only minimally in plumage coloration, with ranges that partly overlap.

1. *E. roseicapillus roseicapillus* (Vieillot)
Characteristics: Size, about 35 cm. Male: Front, crest, lores, and occiput white interspersed with pink; wings, back, and tail gray; cheek area, ear coverts, and nape rosy red; breast and belly pink; lower belly and under tail coverts pale gray; reddish carunculate eye ring; beak horn-colored; feet gray; iris dark brown to black. Female: Similar in coloration to the male, but with a less pronounced eye ring and a red brown iris. Young birds of both sexes have a dark iris and can be recognized by the brown iris color from the second year on.
Distribution: Central and northern Australia.

2. *E. r. assimilis* (Mathews)
Characteristics: Paler plumage than the nominate form; crest more strongly suffused with pink; the naked eye ring is gray white.
Distribution: Western Australia.

Life in the Wild Galahs are distributed over the entire Australian continent and are part of the everyday sights for travelers in Australia. Usually they will be seen in small groups or flocks, but assemblages of several hundred or even a thousand animals are no rarity. As they prefer open areas, they are usually found in savannas and open grasslands, less often in coastal or montane regions. Galahs follow cultivation, and their total population, as well as their range, continues to grow. Extensive cereal cultivation and the construction of watering places by cattle breeders produce a favorable environment for these cockatoos, which are not protected by law except in the

E. r. roseicapillus, female

Galah,
Eolophus roseicapillus

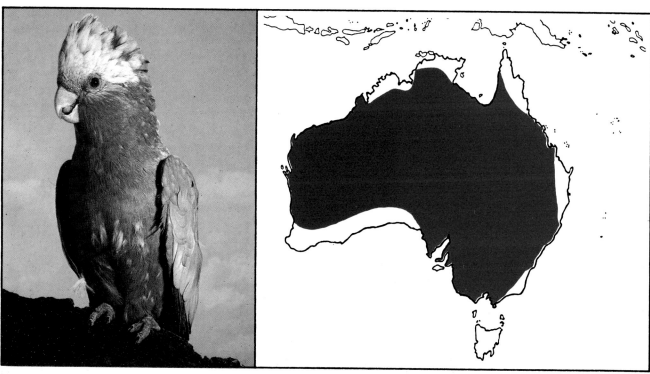

Galahs (**E. r. assimilis**) like to rest on telephone poles and wires. Not infrequently, they are responsible for service interruptions.

cased in wire mesh to keep the animals from breeding. In this manner, they are forced toward the coast in many areas, and in many cities, they are already part of the daily scene. In some places, they are already breeding in yards and parks. In the interior, they are often held responsible for failures in the telegraph network, a preferred resting place, as are fences. Here they do all kinds of stunts, hanging head downward, then rising again and flying to feeding places. Their flight is rapid, with rhythmic wingbeats; they also soar masterfully and, according to my own observations, are capable of hovering for a brief time, like falcons.

They rarely seek food in trees, where they occasionally bite off leaves or pieces of bark; trees

Female Galah (**E. r. roseicapillus**) at the nest entrance. Photographed in the southern part of New South Wales.

Northern Territory; in some cases, they may be hunted even during the breeding season. The damage done by Galahs to the harvest is considerable. Though this is offset in part by their great predilection for weed seeds, no especially fertile imagination is needed to picture the desolation after a flock of several hundred birds has attacked a grain field. Since they also eat grass seeds—estimates say that five thousand of these animals eat thirty tons of these seeds annually—they turn not only the farmers but also the cattle breeders into implacable enemies. The cockatoos are shot and poisoned by the thousands. The fact that the Australian government still does not permit a certain number of these animals to be captured and exported is justified because such an undertaking would be difficult to control; there is a great danger that rarer parrot species would be mixed in and exported.

In some areas of Australia, tree trunks are en-

are usually used only for resting and sleeping. They prefer to eat on the ground, often with other cockatoos, e.g., the Sulphur-crested *(C. galerita)*, Little Corella *(C. sanguinea)*, or Major Mitchell's *(C. leadbeateri)*. When in the company of the Sulphur-crested, they react to the warning system of that species and immediately fly to safety when an enemy approaches. In open country, they cover large distances in rapid flight before settling in another place to feed. They spend many hours in the morning and the late afternoon foraging on the ground, moving around with a waddling gait. Their diet consists of grass seeds predominantly, but the green shoots, roots, and leaves of cabbage plants are also eaten. Insects and larvae meanwhile discovered are a welcome delicacy. Sprouting wheat, like the ripe ears, also appeals to them. There have been repeated observations of Galahs attacking the harvest already in bags.

Because of their large range it is not possible to speak of a definite breeding season. It is determined by the climatic events. With the onset of rain, vegetation grows, and this in turn is the prerequisite for rearing young. In southern Australia, the breeding season usually lasts from July to December, but clutches have been found in February. In the north, the time for reproduction usually follows the rainy season; most nests here are found between February and May. In the interior, rain is the sole triggering factor.

The nest is usually in a hollow tree, predominantly in *Eucalyptus* trees that stand near water, but Galah eggs have been found in rock crevices and even in rabbit holes. Both parents prepare the cavity. Often holes at low heights are chosen, which can be looked into from above without assistance. They may be only 40 cm. deep, with an interior diameter of less than 20 cm. If we view the availability of suitable breeding sites in relation to the number of breeding pairs, this behavior becomes understandable. If a nesting hole which has not been used by other cockatoos of the same species has been chosen, the pair immediately

begin to bite off the bark below the entrance. As incubation progresses, the entire trunk below the hole is stripped and, in some cases, even polished with the dust of the powder downs. If the tree grows at an angle, only the upper side is polished; on a vertical tree, the entire circumference of the trunk is stripped of bark and "waxed." The lower the site of the breeding cavity, the more thorough the treatment. This innate behavior can serve only to protect themselves and the brood from enemies. Climbing the tree is made more difficult, if not altogether impossible.

Both mates participate in this activity, which lasts for several days and is often interrupted by the courtship display of the male. This is as simple as can be, yet impressive. With forceful striding movements and crest erect—the head swings slightly from side to side—the male courts the female, which flies up and is immediately pursued by the cock. After a short acrobatic courtship flight—twittering courtship calls can be heard meanwhile—they both alight on different branches, and the whole display begins again.

As the breeding mood intensifies, both animals carry leaves and small twigs into the nesting hole and prepare a substrate about 10–20 cm. thick. This behavior is explained by the low humidity in central Australia; green vegetation is carried in to provide the humidity necessary for the young to hatch. The clutch, which consists of three to five eggs (averaging 35.5 × 26.5 mm.), is incubated by both mates in turn. The incubation period lasts an average of twenty-five days. During the first days after hatching, the chicks are fed by both parents at intervals of about three hours; begging and feeding sounds can be heard from far away. In addition to food carried in the crop, fly maggots that soon develop in the droppings and the nest are eaten and fed. As the young grow, there is often not enough room for all of them at the bottom of the breeding cavity, and they are fed at the entrance of the nest, usually by turns and with less frequency. The young birds leave the nest at the age of about six weeks, but are cared for by their parents for an additional three to four weeks.

Keeping Galahs came to the London Zoo in 1843 and were imported with increasing frequency from then on. They have always been very popular as cage and aviary birds, especially if they have been taken young from the nest and reared by hand, for then they are remarkably lovable, affectionate parrots that learn many tricks and can even speak moderately well. As a rule, their voice is not particularly loud, and so this beautiful cockatoo can be kept in outdoor aviaries even in neighborhoods where other species would provoke the wrath of the neighbors. Only early in the morning and in the evening will the voices of these animals be heard; very few individuals of this species are loud, noisy birds.

While in Australia Galahs are usually kept as tame pets in cages, here they are definitely considered aviary birds, and not only because of their high price. If their strong need for gnawing is taken into consideration and they are kept in an aviary built of metal, they are pleasant birds that are not very sensitive to being wintered in an unheated shelter room. In the dimensions and furnishings of the aviary, it should be remembered that the animals fly extremely well and like to spend the day on the ground. For this reason, an earth floor is preferable to concrete in every case. All kinds of wild seeds may be sown here to provide welcome enrichment to the diet of the cockatoos during the summer months. Naturally, this entails the danger of infestation by endoparasites; Galahs more often than other species suffer from threadworms and roundworms; regular tests of the droppings by an animal-health laboratory and worming, if necessary, will take care of this. Galahs are said to have been successfully kept at liberty, but in the author's opinion this is an unnecessary risk.

Particularly in recent years, the Galah has been brought in by several German importers;

the author repeatedly saw shipments that sometimes contained more than a hundred animals in excellent condition. Since the exportation of birds from Australia is prohibited, in all cases these are animals that have been smuggled by way of Bangkok. The price nowadays is still correspondingly high, although breeding them is not difficult, given a good diet and care.

Feeding Sunflower seed and teazle, sprouted when possible during the summer months, constitute the basic food; domestic grains soaked overnight, as well as mixed millets and canary seed are taken. As many kinds of fruit and vegetables as possible should be offered; this way, one can tell quickly what they like to eat. Often fruit is not accepted outside of the breeding season; in this case, adding vitamins to the sprouts is recommended. Administration via the water is inadequate because Galahs, as inhabitants of arid regions, drink only sparingly.

Breeding For breeding, it is best to offer hollow logs about 60 cm. high and with an interior diameter of 25–30 cm., which will readily be accepted. The first breeding of Galahs is said to have occurred in London in 1876; nowadays, breeding success is no longer rare, so that in Germany there is already a good breeding stock, and it needs to be further increased. With the revision of the Washington Convention (CITES), no future imports can be expected. In recent years, several German bird fanciers have reported breeding successes in which even newly imported cockatoos proceeded to reproduce successfully the next year.

Since in the wild the animals carry in nesting material, fresh twigs must be offered at all times, particularly during the breeding season; willow twigs are the most suitable. During the sixties, when the necessary experience was still lacking, repeated observations told of animals that carried in spray millet and small pebbles. The twigs not only prepare a microclimate suitable for hatching in the breeding cavity, but also serve as an important stimulus and increase

In flight, Galahs (*E. r. roseicapillus*) constantly make piercing contact calls to keep the flock together.

the animals' inclination to breed. Often as early as March the pair begin to construct the nest, and between April and May, two to five eggs are laid on the substrate and are incubated by both adults in turn. In the literature, the incubation period is indicated as lasting from twenty-one to twenty-nine days; according to personal observation; it lasts for twenty-three days. From the start, the chicks are fed by both parents, as even an uninformed observer can hear from a distance of several meters. Nest inspection usually is not resented; imported animals are more sensitive to this than specimens bred domestically.

If problems occur in the course of rearing the young, Cockatiels *(N. hollandicus)* are particularly good foster parents during the first days of life, since both species use the same feeding technique. During such fostering, the adequacy of feeding should be checked continually; if necessary, feeding must be augmented by means of a feeding utensil. The nestlings leave the nest at about seven weeks and eat on their own about four to five weeks later. Nevertheless, separating the young too early from their parents is not recommended, because the coming weeks play a special role in socialization.

Two successive breedings in one year have occured repeatedly. Galahs have been crossed with the Gang-gang Cockatoo *(C. fimbriatum)*, the Sulphur-crested Cockatoo *(C. galerita)*, the Lesser Sulphur-crested Cockatoo *(C. sulphurea)*, Major Mitchell's Cockatoo *(C. leadbeateri)*, and the Little Corella *(C. sanguinea)*; hybrids with the last two species have also been observed in the wild.

Genus *CACATUA* Vieillot 1817 — white cockatoos

Eleven species All so-called white cockatoos belong to this genus; as the name indicates, their main color is white, occasionally yellowish or faintly salmon-colored. Their distribution extends from the Philippines, Celebes, the Moluccas and the Sunda Islands to New Guinea and the Solomons, with each island group usually having only one species. But on the Australian continent, including Tasmania, four species are found, with ranges that partly overlap. Here speciation must have taken place when the different groups were still living in isolation from one another. Several attempts have been made to divide the genus into subgenera based on differences in the shape of the crest; however, no solution is satisfactory since, because of the great variability, similarities linking the various crest shapes can be put in order only with difficulty. Any distinction of the so-called white-beaked and black-beaked cockatoos is also omitted here, since beak coloration alone does not offer any compelling conclusions about relationships.

Major Mitchell's Cockatoo
Cacatua leadbeateri
(Vigors) 1813

German: *Inkakakadus*
French: *Cacatoès de Leadbeater*
Dutch: *Inca-Kaketoe*

Two subspecies Hall distinguishes two subspecies varying in body size and crest coloration.

1. *C. leadbeateri leadbeateri* (Vigors)
Characteristics: Size, about 38 cm; top of head white with narrow forward-curving crest; crest feathers scarlet red with white tips and yellow middle band; forehead, head, nape, breast, and upper belly salmon pink; under tail coverts, back, and tail white; underside of the primaries and secondaries pink; beak horn-colored; legs

gray; iris dark brown in the male, red in the female. Young birds have paler plumage; the iris of the female becomes red brown in the second year.
Distribution: Arid and semi-arid regions in the interior of Australia, excepting the northeastern part of the continent.

2. *C. l. mollis* (Mathews)
Characteristics: Smaller than the nominate form; crest dark red with only a weakly marked or absent yellow band.
Distribution: The exact distribution of this subspecies is not known; presumably it occurs in southwestern Australia.

Life in the Wild Major Mitchell's Cockatoos inhabit sparsely wooded grasslands in the interior of Australia; this beautiful cockatoo was discovered here in 1830 by the explorer Sir Thomas Mitchell. Forested areas and the

C. l. mollis, female

Major Mitchell's Cockatoo,
Cacatua leadbeateri

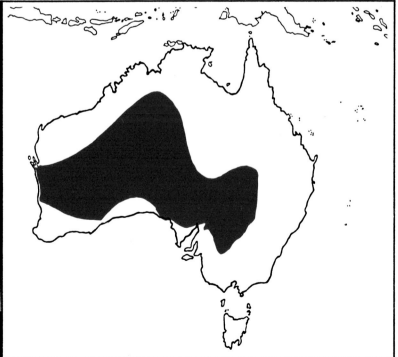

coastal regions of the continent are avoided. Throughout their range they rarely occur in large numbers; they are mostly seen roaming about in pairs or in small groups. Their numbers have diminished considerably in recent years, mainly because of habitat destruction. As the clearing of scrubland progresses, they have become rare, especially in the eastern part of the continent. Large congregations are now an uncommon occurrence. In the dry bed of the Finke River in 1974, Immelmann saw a flock of more than fifty of these magnificent cockatoos, yet even in the years 1978 and 1979, flocks of several hundred of these animals still were sighted occasionally in northwestern Victoria and southwestern Queensland. Such observations, however, are entirely based on chance; if one wants to observe Major Mitchell's Cockatoo in the wild, it most likely will be found in the national parks. The Wyperfeld National Park in northwestern Victoria is one such place that offers the possibility of observation in the wild to the interested observer. The species is protected by law in all states; it may be captured and kept only under a special permit from the wildlife authorities. Illegally kept animals are confiscated and released into the wild.

These cockatoos spend the greater part of the day on the ground, searching for food. Prof. Immelmann observed them eating a native cucumber plant *(Cucumis myriocarpus);* the fruits are held in the foot, and the seeds are picked out with the beak. At this time the animals are said to be extremely aggressive; there are frequent quarrels. Their excitement is indicated by raising the crest and spreading the wings, flashing the salmon pink undersides. Immelmann notes that there is a peck order within a group, so that each animal knows exactly against which it must defend its food and to which it must yield without fighting. Seeds of wild melons *(Citrullus lanatus)* are also eaten, but mainly grass seeds, fruits, nuts, berries, and roots.

Major Mitchell's Cockatoos never remain in one place for long; their presence always depends on the availability of food and water.

They will stay in one place only in the less arid regions. If they are disturbed, they immediately take flight with loud shrieking, but they soon settle to the ground again. Major Mitchell's Cockatoos fly with deep beats of their wings, interrupted by short glides. They are rarely seen at great altitudes; upon landing, the crest is always raised.

The breeding season lasts from August to December; a breeding pair will return year after year to its breeding cavity in a tall hollow tree. The courtship resembles that of the Sulphur-crested Cockatoo; the erect crest functions as an important stimulus key. The head is turned with jerky movements from side to side, and the wings are partly or completely spread so that the colorful underside can be seen. On a substrate of mulch and strips of bark taken from around the entrance to the nest, the female lays three eggs, as a rule (averaging 39.0 × 29.5 mm.), which are incubated by both birds for thirty days. The nestling period is said to last for only six weeks; such a short period of development might be explained by the hard climatic conditions. During the brief periods of vegetation growth that follow the rains, the young must become independent as quickly as at all possible. They remain with their parents for a long while and roam about with them in quest of food.

Keeping Because of their beauty, Major Mitchell's Cockatoos are very much in demand. In 1834, the English naturalist Leadbeater brought them to the London Zoo for the first time, and since then they have been imported repeatedly, but never in large numbers. Since the Australian export ban, they have become a decided rarity, and very high prices are paid for those birds that are smuggled out. Major Mitchell's Cockatoo nowadays has become something of a status symbol; however, it should be kept only by experienced bird fanciers. Only young animals that have been reared by hand will become tame and affectionate toward their keeper; animals caught in the wild usually stay shy for as long as they live and are not suited to being kept in a cage. Because of their rarity, even in their native land, it would be wise to house them in an aviary and to attempt to breed them. Only metal construction and thick wire mesh will withstand their extremely strong beaks. Acclimated animals adjust to our climate very well; in winter, however, they should have a shelter room at their disposal. Since Major Mitchell's Cockatoos are very aggressive, they can be kept only in pairs; if they are kept with other cockatoos, fights will occur sooner or later. In housing Major Mitchell's Cockatoos, consideration should be given to the fact that this species is an especially preferred target of thieves.

Feeding Sunflower seed, teazle, all kinds of cereal grains and small seeds, fresh or cooked corn, and also nuts and various berries and weeds will be accepted; fruits and carrots are usually taken only during the breeding season, but once the animals are accustomed to them, they will eat them regularly from then on. Fresh twigs should always be available for gnawing.

Breeding Because of their rarity, efforts to breed these beautiful cockatoos have always been made, and relatively often have been crowned with success. Especially in recent years, fewer reports of breeding success have been published (though in the late seventies and early eighties this species was imported repeatedly); certainly this stems from caution on the part of the bird fanciers in question. The author knows of several successful breedings in Germany in 1981; the breeders avoid publicity because of their fear of theft. A pair kept in Vogelpark Walsrode also was successful in 1981; a bird that had previously been kept singly in an apartment was paired and two young were reared the following spring.

The first successful breeding was reported by Mrs. Johnstone in England in 1901. Her pair bred in a tree trunk 2.4 m. long and reared three young. Further breedings in England, Belgium, Denmark, East Germany, and South Africa followed. Success was greatest at the San Diego Zoo in California; between 1932 and 1970, fifty-six Major Mitchell's Cockatoos were produced there; however, all animals were reared by hand. They usually were taken from the nest between the fifteenth and twentieth day. Their eyes began to open at about twenty days, and the first feather shafts became visible between the twenty-fifth and twenty-seventh day. By the age of seven weeks, the nestlings were already fully feathered.

The most success in Germany was had by Brechenmacher of Nuremberg, who received four unpaired animals in May of 1964. For a nest box, an oaken barrel was fastened to an iron support high in the shelter room of the aviary (2.50 × 2.50 m.). If tree trunks are used for nesting, they should be hardwood and at least 1 m. tall; young have been reared successfully on a floor area 20 cm. in diameter. Brechenmacher reports an incubation period of only twenty-one to twenty-two days; the male incubated during the day, the female at night. The nestlings developed rapidly; already at four weeks the crest feathers were visible. At the age of seven weeks, the young animals were already being fed at the entrance to the nest box; they fledged at eight weeks. During one visit in the middle seventies, the author was able to admire more than fifteen of these beautiful cockatoos, most of which were said to be descendants of one breeding pair. The female of the best breeding pair had also originally been kept in an apartment as a tame single bird. Apparently, it is easier to breed tame animals.

Lesser Sulphur-crested Cockatoo
Cacatua sulphurea
(Gmelin) 1788

German: *Kleiner Gelbhaubenkakadu,*
   Gelbwangenkakadu
French: *Petit Cacatoès à huppe jaune*
Dutch: *Kleine Geelkuif Kaketoe*

Six subspecies The six subspecies differ mainly in size and in the color of the crest and cheek patches. The orange red variants are less frequently available in the trade than the yellow-crested forms and are therefore more in demand by bird fanciers. Even within the various subspecies differences in size can be noted; if the place of origin is not known, identification is almost impossible.

1. *C. sulphurea sulphurea* (Gmelin)
Characteristics: Size, about 34 cm.; plumage mostly white, occasionally with a yellow tinge; pointed crest and ear patch yellow; under wing coverts and under tail coverts strongly colored with yellow; naked whitish eye ring; beak gray black; feet gray. Males may be recognized by the black iris, which is red in females. Young birds have lighter feet and beaks; young females often may be recognized already in the first year by the brownish iris; iris fully colored in three to four years.
Distribution: Celebes and Butung.

2. *C. s. djampeana* Hartert
Characteristics: Like the nominate form, but with a smaller beak.
Distribution: Djampea and neighboring islands.

C. s. parvula(?), male

Lesser Sulphur-crested Cockatoo,
Cacatua sulphurea

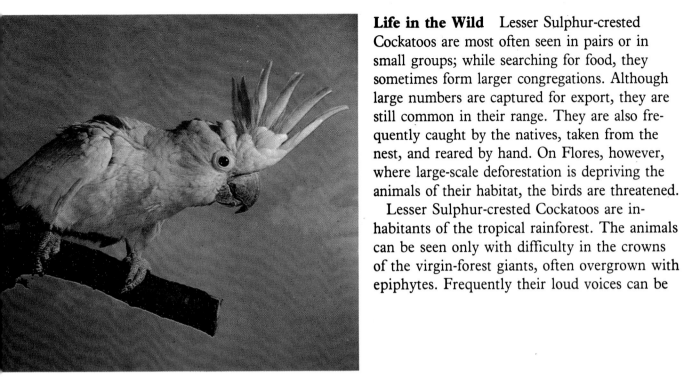

Lesser Sulphur-crested Cockatoo (*C. sulphurea*). Subspecific identification is not possible from this photograph.

Life in the Wild   Lesser Sulphur-crested Cockatoos are most often seen in pairs or in small groups; while searching for food, they sometimes form larger congregations. Although large numbers are captured for export, they are still common in their range. They are also frequently caught by the natives, taken from the nest, and reared by hand. On Flores, however, where large-scale deforestation is depriving the animals of their habitat, the birds are threatened.

Lesser Sulphur-crested Cockatoos are inhabitants of the tropical rainforest. The animals can be seen only with difficulty in the crowns of the virgin-forest giants, often overgrown with epiphytes. Frequently their loud voices can be

Lesser Sulphur-crested Cockatoo (*C. s. citrinocristata*).

3. *C. s. abbotti* (Oberholser)
Characteristics: Pale yellow ear patches; plumage less suffused with yellow.
Distribution: Solombo Besar Island in the Java Sea.

4. *C. s. occidentalis* Hartert
Characteristics: Coloration same as *abbotti*, but smaller.
Distribution: Lombok, Sumbawa, and Flores.

5. *C. s. parvula* (Bonaparte)
Characteristics: Like *occidentalis*, but with a smaller beak; 31 cm.
Distribution: Timor and Semau.

6. *C. s. citrinocristata* (Fraser)
Characteristics: Like *occidentalis*, but crest and cheek patches orange.
Distribution: Sumba.

heard from far away, yet not a single bird can be seen. In addition, the birds are extremely shy; only in the vicinity of corn fields do they sometimes leave the forest. In the mornings, they fly out together in search of food and to waterholes; every evening they seek out the same roosting trees.

Dr. H. Strunden of Essen observed Lesser Sulphur-crested Cockatoos of the subspecies *C. s. occidentalis* on Komodo, a rocky volcanic island famed for the indigenous Komodo dragons, which are threatened by extinction. On the island, which lies between Flores and Sumbawa, the principal locales of the subspecies, he frequently saw small groups of these animals in the lowlands. Whether Komodo was part of the original range or whether the cockatoos were brought here and released by humans could not readily be determined. On Sumba, Lesser Sulphur-crested Cockatoos occur only in the western part of this hilly island, which is 220 km. long and 70 km. wide. Densely forested and traversed by many rivers, its prevailing climate is not as constantly arid as is the other part. Strunden reports that several cockatoos of the subspecies *C. s. citrinocristata* were offered at prices from DM 30–60 in the market of the small "capital," Waingapu. The Sumbanese like to keep these parrots as tame pets, since they are easily trained.

The main breeding season lies between September and October, but clutches have also been found in December. As a rule, three eggs (averaging 41 × 27 mm.) are laid and are incubated by both adults for twenty-four days; the nestling period lasts for ten weeks.

Keeping Nowadays, as before, these cockatoos are not uncommon in the trade. They have become rarer only since the 1981 revision of the Washington Convention (CITES); as a rule, the Indonesian government no longer issues export papers for this species. The author himself noticed that many birds originating in Indonesia are sold there at higher prices than here, since capturing and keeping them is prohibited. Many cockatoos, as well as lories and ring-necked parakeets, that are offered for sale in Europe have been smuggled to Singapore and shipped from there. However, the export papers and certificates of origin issued by that island state are no longer recognized by the authorities.

Of all the cockatoo species, the Lesser Sulphur-crested Cockatoos are the most suited to being kept in a cage. If obtained young, they usually quickly become tame and allow every visitor to scratch their feathers. Because of their size, they are also satisfied with less space, and flying feather dust dirtying the furniture is also kept in bounds. They learn all kinds of tricks, and, based on my own observations, some specimens can even talk quite well. Older animals, on the other hand, always remain reticent; they make hissing noises of intimidation when approached, meanwhile raising their crest. Caring for such animals soon becomes tiresome; they are better suited to an aviary and breeding. The responsibility assumed with the purchase of such a cockatoo should be made clear. If a hand-reared young animal is bought, it will be very tame from the beginning and will soon establish a close rapport with its keeper. The need for contact in such animals is especially great; they really need to have a lot of time devoted to them. If the thrill of the novelty is lost after a few weeks, these pitiful creatures often become shriekers and thereby so-called "wandering birds," with constantly changing owners. Pairing them will also often cause difficulties; imprinted on humans, usually they will no longer accept a conspecific. Put into an aviary, it often takes a very long time until they make friends with their mate.

Aviary keeping is always preferable, although these cockatoos have successfully reared young in larger cages in an apartment. They are comparatively hardy animals that on occasion have been wintered in the cold in outdoor aviaries without suffering any damage; in the following year, they again successfully reared young. In the author's opinion, however, this is certainly not the correct way to keep this species; the animals should at least have the option of a frost-free shelter room.

Feeding Teazle, sunflower seed, domestic grains, millet, and hemp are taken. Small nuts, berries, and various kinds of fruits and vegetables are also enjoyed, once the animals are accustomed to them. Fresh twigs for gnawing should be available, especially if the construction of the aviary is not particularly sturdy.

Breeding Breeding first succeeded for M. T. Allen in England; in 1920, two young hatched but soon died, however. In 1924, two young hatched from three eggs; one egg was infertile. One month after the two young cockatoos had left the nest, one was killed by the male. Such attacks are not uncommon in cockatoos and presumably must be seen as aberrant behavior caused by captivity. Careful observation is advisable, and perhaps early separation, if the parents become inclined to breed again.

Since then, many reports of successful breedings of this species can be found in the literature. In Switzerland alone, according to the stock list, various bird fanciers had reared more than fifty youngsters by 1981; not only the nominate form, but also the more desirable "Citron-crested" Cockatoos nowadays regularly rear young in captivity. If a pair are in good condition, they will, as a rule, proceed to breed without problems. The large number of breeding successes should be viewed in terms of the fact that very likely this species is the one most widely kept.

Once we have a harmonious pair, housing seems to play a subordinate role as far as a breeding success is concerned. Lesser Sulphur-crested Cockatoos have time and again been bred in room cages, often no larger than one cubic meter. Especially in such situations, but even in an aviary, it is an advantage if the animals are somewhat tame; inspections and disturbances are less likely to be resented. On the other hand, the author knows a tame pair of Lesser Sulphur-crested Cockatoos that regularly left the eggs when their keeper approached, in order to let themselves be petted at the cage wires.

A breeding cage should be at least large enough to permit the nesting hole to be installed inside. A nest box fastened to the cage from the outside is less readily accepted. In the choice of a nest, these cockatoos are not fussy; a wooden box built of rough boards serves the same purpose as a tree trunk. The interior dimensions should be 25–30 cm.; a depth of 50 cm. is sufficient. During the day, both animals will often sit in the nest, because the tireless search for food by the nonincubating mate is unnecessary in captivity. It is advisable to situate the box in the darkest possible corner of the cage or shelter room, since Lesser Sulphur-crested Cockatoos are forest dwellers; even in the wild, they like to nest where the light is dim. Similar observations can be made for many parrots living in forests; often the breeding cavity is accepted only after the entrance is turned away from the light.

Usually courtship already can be observed in early spring. The male circles the female with hopping movements; frequent forward bows with crest raised indicate readiness to mate. If the cockatoos are kept in a heated room, they may breed in the fall and winter months. As a rule, two or three eggs are laid; incubation lasts for twenty-four days (for "Citron-crested" Cockatoos, twenty-eight days is reported in the literature). The young are reared by both parents and leave the nest after nine or ten weeks. The nestling period is certainly related to the diet; if more animal protein is fed, the nestlings grow more quickly and leave the nest earlier. Fresh corn on the cob, peas, dandelions, and other weeds are usually taken gladly during this time, even though the animals refused all green food previously. After leaving the nest the young will continue to beg for food for three to four weeks.

Sulphur-crested Cockatoo
Cacatua galerita
(Latham) 1790

German: *Grosser Gelbhaubenkakadu*
French: *Cacatoès à crête jaune*
Dutch: *Grote Geelkuif Kaketoe*

Four subspecies Forshaw describes and names four subspecies, which differ mainly in size. Other authors list as many as eight subspecies. In the opinion of the author, it is not sufficiently clear whether these are merely geographical races; their ranges, which are only slightly separate, suggest this.

1. *C. galerita galerita* (Latham)
Characteristics: Size, about 50 cm.; plumage mostly white; ear patches yellowish; forward-curving narrow yellow crest; undersides of wing and tail feathers yellow; naked white eye ring; beak gray black; legs dark gray; iris dark brown to black. At two or three years of age, females can be recognized by the reddish brown iris; young animals resemble the adult male, but often have a pale gray tinge to the plumage.
Distribution: Northern, eastern, and southern Australia, from the Cape York Peninsula to and including Tasmania and King Island.

2. *C. g. fitzroyi* (Mathews)
Characteristics: Somewhat smaller than the nominate form; more yellow in the plumage of the head; naked eye ring often pale blue; beak broader and duller than the nominate form.
Distribution: Northern Australia, from the Fitzroy River to the Gulf of Carpentaria.

3. *C. g. triton* Temminck
Characteristics: Size, about 45 cm.; yellow cheek patches absent; naked blue eye ring; crest shorter and broader than that of the nominate form.
Distribution: New Guinea and some nearby islands.

C. g. fitzroyi, male

Sulphur-crested Cockatoo,
Cacatua galerita

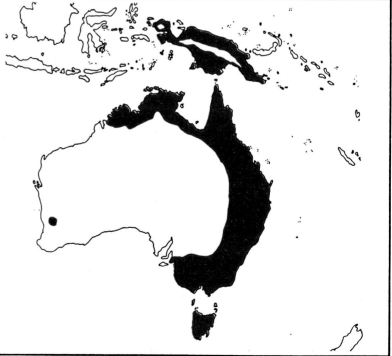

Mixed growth of eucalypts and grassy trees of the lily family in the Atherton Tableland in northeastern Australia. Toward the west, this borders dry eucalyptus savannah. The Sulphur-crested Cockatoo (*C. g. galerita*) occurs in both types of habitat.

4. *C. g. eleonora* Finsch
Characteristics: In coloration and size like *triton*, but with a smaller, narrower beak.
Distribution: Aru Islands.

Life in the Wild Sulphur-crested Cockatoos are inhabitants of open woodland; they are most often observed in trees near watercourses, but also can be found in the mangrove swamps of the Gulf of Carpentaria and in the tropical rainforest of the Cape York Peninsula. These loud, noisy cockatoos are an everyday occur-rence in their range. When eating, but also dur-ing preening and in flight, they constantly make shrill cries, so that they are easy to discover. During the breeding season, they usually wander about in pairs or family groups. At other times, flocks of several hundred are not uncommon; however, this is true only for the Australian subspecies. In 1970 at the Mur-ray River, A. Preussiger observed a flock of over five thousand of these animals. In southern Australia, where they prefer open country, their warning system can be well observed. Single animals will always sit nearby on high perches while the others are searching for food on the ground. If danger approaches, the sentinel flys up with loud cries, and the entire flock takes off. According to Forshaw, this warning system is not used in northern Australia, where the cockatoos predominantly live in the trees.

Sulphur-crested Cockatoos are usually sedentary; every group has its regular resting and feeding places. If a flock alights in the crown of a tree standing alone, from a distance it looks as if the tree were covered with blossoms. Because of their deafening shrieking, however, the animals can be detected from far off. Such roosting trees, which are usually dead, serve not only for resting during the hot midday but also as sleeping places every evening. Often branches will break under the weight of the large animals. At sunrise, the cockatoos leave the sleeping trees to fly to the feeding places and waterholes. Agricultural expansion continues to extend the range of the Sulphur-crested Cockatoos. Food is usually sought on the ground; the seeds of all available grasses and wild herbs are eaten; berries, fruits, roots, and also insects are consumed. Cockatoos have been observed digging for grasshopper eggs. Nevertheless, the animals are not liked by farmers and cattle ranchers, and they are sometimes persecuted unmercifully, though they are protected the year around. They cause great damage to wheat, corn, and peanut crops, especially if they appear in large numbers. They eat only a part of the fruiting head and carelessly let the greater part fall to the ground, where it rots. For drinking, the animals prefer sandy river banks.

The breeding season varies according to locality. In southern Australia it lasts from August to January, in the north from May to September. In southern New Guinea, occupied nests were found in November, but the main breeding season in the northern part of the island appears to lie between February and May. Breeding cavities are usually found in tall *Eucalyptus* and rubber trees, but occasionally this species will breed in crevices among rocks.

The subspecies living on New Guinea and the surrounding islands are forest dwellers and usually are observed only in small groups. Their feathers are often used in headdresses by the natives.

Courtship is simple and brief. With crest erect and vigorous, showy steps, the male marches toward the female, meanwhile making soft chirping sounds. As excitement increases, the head is jerkily turned back and forth. Episodes of social grooming are often included. The female lays two or rarely three eggs (averaging 45.5 × 33.0 mm.), which are incubated for twenty-nine days by both parents in turn. Usually loud, the animals are very quiet during incubation in order to not attract their natural enemies, lizards and snakes, to the breeding cavity. The nestling period is said to last for about six weeks; afterward, parents and young join the flock that forms again after breeding.

Keeping Because of its impressive demeanor, the Sulphur-crested Cockatoo is a popular cage bird even in Australia. If obtained young, the animals usually become tame quickly, but often are affectionate only with certain people. Even nowadays they still are seen in circus or variety acts, where they perform all kinds of tricks. While the forms indigenous to Australia seldom reach us because of the export regulations, *triton* is imported regularly, if not in large numbers. Accordingly, this cockatoo, together with the Lesser Sulphur-crested Cockatoo (*C. sulphurea*), is one of the species most frequently kept in cages or on stands. Because they are sedentary, they can be kept at liberty; Konrad Lorenz reports such experiments. They also enjoy undiminished popularity in zoos. In captivity these robust animals often attain a very old age. Some specimens are reported to have lived more than one hundred years.

Males usually become tame more quickly than females, which often remain distrustful and shy all their lives. The disadvantages that accompany keeping such a cockatoo should be mentioned here. As a rule, Sulphur-crested Cockatoos are very loud; in the early morning especially, they let their strong voices be heard. Being sociable birds, if left alone they often develop into screamers. Sooner or later, the noise will become so insupportable that they will be given away, despite their affection and tameness. Thus, there are at least forty birds living together peacefully in a large aviary in the Adelaide Zoo; most of them were "gifts" from disappointed fanciers.

Although they have laid eggs several times, there has never been a successful breeding yet, nor has firm pair bonding been observed. This accords with field observations: when the animals are ready to breed, they separate from the flock; only then will breeding proceed without hindrance. Accordingly, in aviaries the cockatoos must be kept separately in pairs if breeding is the goal. An aviary constructed to withstand their strong beaks is a prerequisite. Although the animals once acclimated are not sensitive to our climate, they should have a shelter room at their disposal, so that they can be closed in during the night. Few neighbors will appreciate their early-morning shrieking. It goes without saying that the nest box must be hung inside. Correctly housed and given a varied diet, the animals will proceed to breed comparatively easily.

Feeding The basic mixture consists of sunflower seed, teazle, wheat, oats, corn, and small seeds such as canary, hemp, and millet. All kinds of weed seeds—freshly collected fruiting heads are best—nuts, berries, and a variety of fruits and vegetables enrich the menu. Oranges, cherries, and grapes are said to be especially enjoyed.

Breeding In Australia few bird fanciers concern themselves with breeding this impressive cockatoo; the reason is certainly because they are so common. In Germany usually the nominate form is kept for breeding purposes. Hollow logs with an inside diameter of about 40 cm. and boxes made of thick boards with

the same interior measurements and 1 m. or more deep are gladly accepted for nesting. Such nest boxes should be installed at a slight angle so that the animals cannot jump right onto the clutch from above.

The first successful breeding was reported by Mme. E. Delaitre in Algiers in 1879. In a cage measuring only 80 × 50 cm., one youngster was reared, and the next year two. The year 1883 saw breeding success in Europe for the first time; a bird fancier near Berlin was successful repeatedly. Breeding reports from England, the U.S.A., and other countries followed, but especially in recent years, reports have declined again, because of the tighter import restrictions. In Germany the most success probably was had by A. Preussiger of Neuwied. Two animals he had owned for several years but which were paired only in 1976 bred successfully the following year. In June, the female laid a single egg in a wooden box measuring 40 × 40 cm. by 1.5 m. high. The nest box was put up at a forty-five degree angle in the outside flight (1.5 × 4.0 m.), while the animals were fed exclusively in the adjoining shelter room (1.5 × 2.0 m.). The egg was incubated by both adults for thirty days; at hatching, the nestling was covered with yellow down and weighed 28 g. During the breeding period, the animals were remarkably quiet and never aggressive toward their owner or the author. Nest inspections were not resented; the nestling could be measured, weighed, and photographed daily. It should be mentioned, however, that the female was hand-tame.

During the first three weeks, the youngster was fed every two hours by both parents; the begging and feeding noises could be heard for some distance. After ten days, the nestling weighed 165 g.; after twenty days, it was almost 450 g. The eyes were beginning to open, and the egg tooth had already fallen off. The first feather shafts of the tail, wing, and back feathers were breaking through the skin. On the fiftieth day, the little cockatoo reached its full weight of 850 g. and was almost com-

Major Mitchell's (*C. leadbeateri*) and Sulphur-crested (*C. galerita*) cockatoos pair readily in captivity, and Australian zoos have repeatedly bred hybirds of the two species.

pletely feathered. When taken from the nest, it hissed and threatened with raised crest. At this time, it was fed only occasionally. During the last three weeks of the eighty-five-day nestling period, the parents fed it only in the evening and morning. A special rearing food was not offered. In addition to the usual seed mixture and dandelion leaves, several carrots were given daily. The young bird was fed by the parents for about ten weeks after fledging. In the following years the pair was repeatedly successful. However, they regularly laid two eggs now and always produced two young.

At present, a pair belonging to W. Heinrich of Mainz is raising a youngster.

Although the *triton* cockatoo is imported much more often, reports of successful breeding are rarer. Among other things this may be due to the fact that this subspecies is not always recognized as such. The first breeding report comes from the Amsterdam Zoo in 1969. In the U.S.A., R. Schock of North Carolina reported the first success in 1975. After a one-month incubation period, a chick hatched on June 19. Its begging noises could be heard a distance of 20 m. It left the nest on September 12, at the age of twelve weeks. In April of the following year the hen laid two eggs, and the young were taken from the nest for hand-rearing in the middle of May. In the mid-1970s, other breeders and zoos in the U.S.A., New Zealand, England, and Germany were also successful. A Swiss bird fancier last bred this species successfully in 1981.

122

Blue-eyed Cockatoo
Cacatua ophthalmica
Sclater 1864

German: *Brillenkakadu*
French: *Cacatoès yeux bleux*
Dutch: ?

The Blue-eyed Cockatoo is closely related to the Sulphur-crested Cockatoo *(C. galerita);* some systematists consider it merely a subspecies of *galerita*. However, in crest shape it resembles the Salmon-crested Cockatoo *(C. moluccensis)* more.

Characteristics: Size, about 45 cm.; plumage mainly white; inner circlet of the long round crest yellow; deep blue naked eye ring; beak, cere, and feet black; iris brown in the male, reddish in the female.

Distribution: New Ireland and New Britain in the Bismarck Archipelago.

Life in the Wild   In the forests of New Britain, the Blue-eyed Cockatoo is not uncommon. It can be found up to altitudes of 1000 m. Flocks of ten to twenty animals assemble at dusk, probably in search of sleeping trees. During flight, the animals make much use of their loud voices, so they cannot be missed even from far away. As a rule, however, these cockatoos are seen in pairs; mates are firmly bonded even outside of the breeding season. So far, there are no detailed observations about the breeding period and their behavior in the wild. Successful breeding in captivity, however, permits certain conclusions to be drawn.

Keeping   Today, as formerly, this cockatoo is a rarity. Because of the ban on its exportation, it comes to us only occasionally. The first

C. ophthalmica

Blue-eyed Cockatoo,
Cacatua ophthalmica

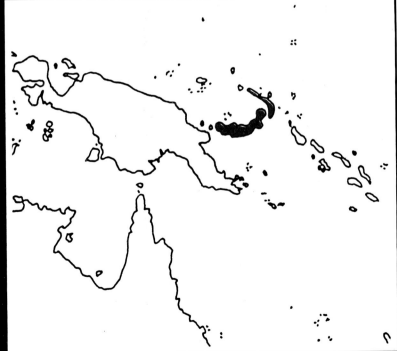

specimens were exhibited in the mid-1860s in the zoos of London and Hamburg. At the moment, Chester Zoo in England and San Diego Zoo own some birds of this little-known species. They are said to be very easy to keep and to become tame readily. Because of their rarity, Blue-eyed Cockatoos should if possible be kept only in pairs and breeding them should be attempted; singly kept animals should be brought together in breeding cooperatives.

Feeding   Sunflower seed, teazle, wheat, oats, and corn, dry or sprouted, and berries and fruit should be offered.

Breeding   If we consider that this cockatoo is hardly ever kept in captivity, the available breeding reports indicate that it is not too difficult to breed. The first breeding succeeded for Sir Edward Hallstrom in 1951 in Australia; the first success known in Europe occurred in 1963. In the same year, a pair imported into Wales, and housed in a large aviary over 10 m. long, came into breeding condition in late summer. In October the first egg was laid, but because of egg binding, this attempt was unsuccessful. From a clutch of two eggs laid in July of the following year, one youngster was reared and left the nest on November 10. In the fall of 1965, another youngster was produced.

Since the main breeding season presumably occurs during our autumn months, the animals must be housed so that they have a shelter room available. Some heat must be provided in case the animals show any inclination to breed. The best nest box is a hollow log with an inside diameter of about 40 cm., at least 1 m. high, installed in the shelter room. Kept only in an outdoor flight with an unheated shelter, the cockatoos are not likely to produce young in our climate; with such accommodations it will be several years before they adjust their breeding cycle to our summer months.

Meanwhile, Blue-eyed Cockatoos have been bred repeatedly in the Chester Zoo in England; as a rule, one or two eggs are laid. There is no

exact information about the incubation period; likely it takes between twenty-eight and thirty days. The nestling period is said to last for four months. In addition to the usual seeds, cooked rice and insect larvae were given. In 1981, a male born in the zoo bred successfully; although this cockatoo was only three years old, the single egg was fertile, and the chick was reared. With the success of the second pair, the group amounted to seven animals altogether.

Salmon-crested Cockatoo
Cacatua moluccensis
(Gmelin) 1788

German: *Molukkenkakadu, Rothaubenkakadu*
French: *Cacatoès à huppe rouge*
Dutch: *Roodkuif-Kaketoe*

Characteristics: Size, about 55 cm.; white plumage with a soft pink to salmon red tinge; round crest of pink-colored outer feathers and a circlet of long, fraying vermilion red feathers behind; beak gray black; feet dark gray; iris dark brown to black; the sexes cannot be differentiated by iris color. Animals vary considerably in size and degree of pink in the plumage; they may eventually be treated as geographical races, or perhaps the variations stem from the foods available for rearing the young. Even young Salmon-crested Cockatoos may be intensely salmon-colored in part, so plumage coloration is no indicator of age.
Distribution: Southern Moluccas: the islands of Ceram, Saparua, and Haruku.

Life in the Wild   Field observations of Salmon-crested Cockatoos are rare. These birds are usually captured by natives and offered for sale or barter to professional animal traders, who are hardly interested in zoological questions. Scientists and travelers interested in science visit the islands only rarely. These conspicuous cockatoos are found mainly in regions near the coast, where they prefer lowlands and hilly country. They have been sighted only occasionally at altitudes above 1000 m. Salmon-crested Cockatoos are forest dwellers, and they prefer to find their food, all kinds of fruits and berries, on trees. Although they often form larger groups in their search for food, the mates of a pair stay close together even within the flock. On Ceram, they plague the coconut plantations, where they feed on the unripe fruits. They also damage corn and grain fields. As a result, probably, they are unprotected and large numbers are captured for export.

Since Salmon-crested Cockatoos prefer very tall nesting trees, the natives can reach the breeding cavities only with difficulty; thus hand-reared young are rare. Only the more accessible breeding trees are "harvested," for several years, as a rule. Year after year, the cockatoos occupy the same tree for rearing their brood. The incubation period is said to last twenty-nine days; the two eggs (averaging 50.0 × 33.5 mm.) are incubated by both parents. There are no field observations available about the nestling period.

Keeping The Salmon-crested Cockatoo is a popular cage and aviary bird. If one gets a young animal, it will quickly become attached to the human and be an absolutely charming pet in respect to tameness and temperament. Keeping them also has drawbacks which must be pointed out. Because of their size, Salmon-crested Cockatoos produce a great amount of oily feather dust, which sooner or later covers all the furniture with a whitish layer. For this reason alone, many a housewife has grown tired of caring for an otherwise pleasant pet. A regular shower has only limited value. Their voices have enormous volume, and the trumpeting calls are delivered mainly in the evening and in the early morning hours. Although some Salmon-crested Cockatoos hardly ever use their strong voices, most are not suited to being kept in a rented apartment. Sooner or later the animal will arouse the

displeasure of the other apartment dwellers. The tamer and more confiding a Salmon-crested Cockatoo is, the less its voice is heard, as a rule. On the other hand, even tame cockatoos can develop into horrible shriekers when neglected, and even the most patient person will be disaffected.

No object in the apartment can withstand their strong beaks. In accordance with their size, they must be housed in a large cage and must be allowed the freedom of the room for some time daily. They feel most comfortable when kept on a stand or a bow perch, but, like daily freedom, this should be supervised. Healthy Salmon-crested Cockatoos will gnaw on all the furniture; even light switches are taken off and electrical wiring torn from the wall. A Salmon-crested Cockatoo known to the author was responsible for more than one short circuit, without suffering any injury itself. The cockatoos' natural need to gnaw can be partially satisfied by giving them fresh branches constantly. But even then, one should keep an eye on them. If their wings are trimmed, they should be put into the yard on a bow perch or a climbing tree for a few hours daily. However, the animals dislike strong sunshine; they should always be able to seek shade.

The optimal housing for these stately birds is an outdoor aviary at least 2 m. wide; here they can use their strong wings, and one will be surprised to see what skillful flyers these apparently clumsy cockatoos are. Salmon-crested Cockatoos should be wintered in a heated shelter room; on nice days, they can be allowed into the outdoor flight. The aviary must be constructed to withstand the strong beaks. When the animals have settled in, within hours they will gnaw through the spot-welded wire mesh customarily used by bird fanciers in aviary construction. A Salmon-crested Cockatoo known to the author completely demolished the wire side wall of a flight in the shortest time; fortunately it ended up in the neighboring flight. Holes were eaten into the walls of the shelter house, which were of pumice stone;

arm-thick perches had to be replaced every three or four days. Generally, the amount of destruction is in inverse proportion to the size of the aviary. Salmon-crested Cockatoos have been kept in outdoor flights of which the wooden frame was covered only with a thin hexagonal wire mesh; however, the area was more than 100 square meters. The need for gnawing is especially great before the breeding period.

Feeding Sunflower seed, domestic grains, all kinds of small seeds and nuts. Even spray millet is eaten gladly, the small seeds being skillfully picked up with the beak. It often takes a longer time to accustom them to fruits and vegetables.

Breeding Although not uncommon in the trade, Salmon-crested Cockatoos have been bred only occasionally thus far. The first youngster was reared by hand in 1951 in the San Diego Zoo. Later attempts by several bird fanciers were still only partial successes, as, for instance, the first breeding in 1972 of the pair acquired by Herr Öhler of Friedrichshafen. A successful natural breeding was long awaited; the pair mentioned reared a single youngster in the late summer of 1977; by the following year it was still not completely feathered, probably due to some deficiency during rearing. The pair meanwhile was sold to another bird lover and since has not proceeded to breed again.

Several months earlier, Prof. G. Andres of Mainz successfully bred the Salmon-crested Cockatoo. A female purchased in the spring of 1962 quickly became tame. The bird lived as a pet with the family until it flew away in August of the same year through the pane of a closed window. Since searching proved fruitless, another cockatoo, a male, was bought in October. The female was caught in early November in a fruit orchard in the vicinity of Mainz. After a short period of adjustment, the

C. moluccensis

Salmon-crested Cockatoo,
Cacatua moluccensis

Colony of Salmon-crested Cockatoos (*C. moluccensis*).

the embryo developed in the incubator for only twelve days. Two months later, another clutch of two eggs was eagerly incubated. Presumably because of the low humidity in the breeding cavity, the young did not hatch. Another clutch followed in December; this time, the young again died in the egg. A chick that hatched in April 1968 after an incubation period of thirty days was killed by the parents. After a change in location of the cages, the female began to pull her feathers and, although she laid several times more, had to be put to sleep in 1970. The bird had begun to tear off her own skin.

A female purchased the following spring was transferred, together with the cock, into an empty kitchen of the house (3.8 × 2.2 × 2.5 m.); a month later the first copulations were observed. In 1975, two eggs were laid at intervals of five days; unfortunately, both embryos again died during incubation. In the fall, the male

Salmon-crested Cockatoo (*C. moluccensis*), 6 weeks old.

animals got along very well, but four years passed before breeding was attempted. The first copulation was observed in April 1967. Invited by the female, the male circled her, making soft cries, before treading. As the cockatoos were copulating more and more often, a nest box was constructed (40 × 40 × 55 cm.) and fastened to the two cages which were placed side by side. During this time, the animals were allowed longer periods of freedom in the apartment.

In May of the same year, the first egg was laid; it measured 48 × 29 mm. and weighed 23 g. It was thrown from the box by the male, and became increasingly aggressive, even attacking the female. Nevertheless, in early January 1976, two eggs lay in the nest. This time, incubation took place without a hitch, and on February 6, the characteristic feeding sounds were heard for the first time. During a nest inspection, two downy white young raised their pale open beaks toward the hand. After eight days the feeding sounds of the young were more differentiated; during feeding they uttered a soft chirping. After eighteen days, the nestlings already were the size of two fists, and during nest inspections, the still-pale beaks were opened wide as hissing noises were made. In early March, the feeding sounds became less obvious; instead, the nestlings begged loudly when one of the parents visited the box. At about six weeks their beaks turned black, and at the age of two months they became increasingly active. Occasionally one youngster would come to the entrance of the nest box, which was standing on the ground, in order to be fed there. On May 5, after a nestling period of exactly ninety days, the first young bird left the box for the first time; the second followed a few days later. Initially, their movements seemed very immature and clumsy. The very slow development necessitates a long period of parental guidance; thus the young were separated from the adults only in September. Further breedings followed. Kept in a home, Salmon-crested Cockatoos apparently are not tied to a definite breeding season. By 1978, a total of seven young animals had been reared. One of them had to be reared by hand, since the father not only pulled its feathers, but had also bitten its head and foot. After that, unfortunately, the breeding cock died.

In recent years, breeding has been successful for other bird fanciers here and abroad. It is remarkable that the breeding pairs are often birds previously kept as household pets. Apparently, it is an advantage if at least one of the breeding pair is tame. Salmon-crested Cockatoos are extremely sensitive animals that are bothered by any disturbance.

White Cockatoo
Cacatua alba
(P. L. S. Müller) 1776

German: *Weisshaubenkakadu*
French: *Cacatoès à huppe blanche*
Dutch: *Witte Kaketoe*

Characteristics: Size, about 40-45 cm.; plumage white with broad, pure white crest; undersides of wing and tail feathers yellow; blue white naked eye ring; feet and beak black; iris black in the male; young females can be recognized already in the first year by the gray brown iris, which will turn red by four years of age; in addition, they are smaller and are easily recognized by the smaller head and beak.
Distribution: Central and northern Moluccas: the islands of Obi, Batjan, Halmahera, Ternate, and Tidore.

Life in the Wild Because of the remoteness of their range, very little is known about the life of these cockatoos in the wild. It is said that they are not uncommon, and they are usually observed in pairs or small groups. If they are searching for food in the branches of tall trees—they feed mainly on berries, fruits, and nuts—they can be detected from far away. White Cockatoos are loud birds, and they also call during flight. When startled, the impressive crest is raised; it also has important signalling functions in courtship. Maximally erected, it makes the bird appear larger; the head feathers are also spread wide, and the wings lifted. With hopping movements, the male dances around the female; soft, unmelodic calls accompany the courtship dance.

As a rule, two eggs are laid (averaging 41 × 33 mm.) and are incubated for twenty-nine days. Unfortunately, very little is known about incubation and nestling periods and breeding behavior in the wild. The climatic uniformity throughout their range suggests that White Cockatoos probably breed during all seasons of the year; this accords with observations in captivity.

Keeping Although not uncommon in the trade, this cockatoo is not particularly popular; therefore, only limited numbers are usually imported. The animals are, considering their size and the associated transportation costs, still advantageously priced. White Cockatoos have never attained the popularity of Salmon-crested Cockatoos because a similar noise level and destructiveness accompanies a comparatively less attractive exterior. Only close observation will reveal the beauty of these impressive birds, which are especially striking in their enormous feather crest. With roomy accommodations and proper care they prove to be hardy birds with few needs. Even among wild-caught birds, there is hardly ever one that will not become tame with correct handling. However, the disadvantages listed for the Salmon-crested Cockatoo hold true for this species too. A wild-caught bird purchased by the author was initially extremely shy, but after three or four weeks the barriers were broken, and the animal permitted its head to be scratched. A typical parrot cage had already been dismantled by this time; the welds were cracked with the mighty beak. After a few weeks, the cockatoo was friendly toward everybody and let even strangers touch it and pet its feathers. Freed from its cage in the evening, the animal immediately sought contact with its keeper. If it was left alone in the room for just a few moments, one often found beak marks on the furniture upon returning. It is virtually impossible to devote the necessary time to such a pet; therefore, although very lovable, the animal was paired. It immediately lost all its tameness. The young reared by this pair were also extremely nice pets; however, they all became attached to one particular person. A young male, normally tame toward everyone, does not let himself be touched in the presence of his keeper; if approached, he will even attack. The attacks are accompanied by continuous intimidation behavior that resembles play behavior, but may end painfully.

Kept in an aviary, White Cockatoos seldom become tame; only unpaired animals will stay trusting. If this is important, both animals must first be tamed in a cage singly before being put together. In the construction of the aviary the destructive power of their beaks should be considered. Especially before the breeding season cockatoos show a very great need for gnawing; the author's pair regularly chewed large holes into a fairly sturdy wire mesh (3 mm. gauge). Even the welds in steel construction mats were cracked and the individual wires pulled out. In planning the aviary, it is best to choose wavy wire mesh from the start.

The animals are extremely aggressive during the breeding period. In several instances, birds in adjoining flights have been attacked, and the quarrels often ended with bloody toes. A Plum-crowned Parrot (*Pionus tumultuosus*) that entered the cockatoo flight through a freshly made hole was immediately killed and torn apart beyond recognition.

Once acclimated, White Cockatoos are extremely hardy birds that can barely be hurt by our climate; nevertheless, they should be wintered frost-free, because their large feet tend to freeze. In addition, they are inclined to start breeding during the winter months.

Feeding Sunflower seed and teazle are the staples of their diet, which should be enriched with small seeds and sprouted domestic grains. Nuts and berries are also relished. Accustoming them to fruit and green food can take years.

Breeding The first breeding success took place for P. Schneider in California in 1960. His pair had lived for four years in a roomy aviary with an area of more than forty square meters. Several times, eggs were laid, but they were usually found broken after a few days. In June 1960, the first youngster was discovered during a nest inspection. The roomy nest box had recently been replaced by a smaller breeding cavity. The nestling period lasted eleven weeks.

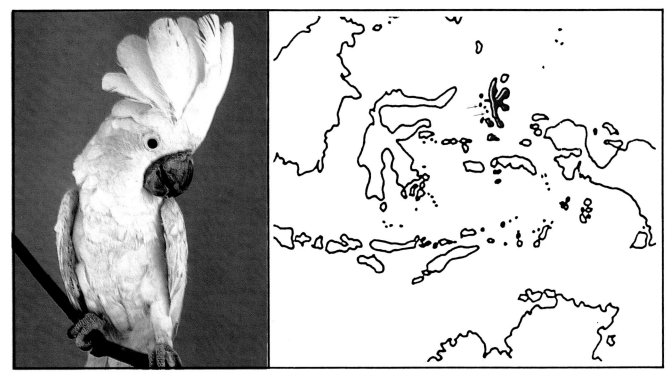

C. alba, male

White Cockatoo,
Cacatua alba

In 1965, a young bird was reared by hand in Denmark; the first natural breeding in Europe succeeded in 1967 at the Rode bird garden in England. Although hundreds of visitors streamed by the aviary everyday, the cockatoos, otherwise so sensitive, reared one youngster. Housed in an aviary 4.3 × 2.5 m., the cockatoos initially were very shy and fled into the nest box at every disturbance. It was almost three years before the first egg was laid; the cockatoos previously had the company of other species but now lived alone in the aviary. Two eggs, deposited in a barrel 40 cm. in diameter and only 50 cm. high, were incubated by both adults. Throughout the incubation period, both animals usually stayed in the nest, which was situated in the roofed-over section of the outdoor flight.

The first breeding in Germany occurred in 1972; two pairs housed in a large communal aviary (20 × 14 × 4 m.) began their courtship display in early March. The first clutch broke. From the second, one chick hatched after an incubation period of thirty-three (?) days; it was taken from the nest after eight weeks and reared by hand.

The author's breeding pair was successful the first year they were paired. The male, after more than two years as a tame pet, was put with a newly purchased female in late summer of 1978. Their new home was a room aviary (2.0 × 3.0 × 2.5 m.). They greeted each other with excited beak clapping, and mutual preening an hour later gave evidence of their compatibility. From this moment on, the male was again just as reticent and shy as when he was purchased. The female, which had been kept with a Salmon-crested Cockatoo for many years, was always shy. Four weeks later, the first copulations were observed, and three months after pairing, in November 1978, laying first took place. A hollow cherry-tree trunk 40 cm.

in diameter and 150 cm. high had its cover gnawed off; both cockatoos threw out all the nesting materials put in for substrate. Probably because of insufficient humidity during incubation, the embryos died. A second clutch followed three weeks later; a youngster hatched after twenty-nine days but was not fed. The third clutch, again two eggs, brought success. In May of 1979, two young cockatoos hatched in accordance with the laying interval of five days. Only the older nestling was fed, and it left the nest after ninety-five days. Feeding noises could be heard from the first day on through the closed door of the room.

No definite information can be given about the development of the nestlings. A second nestling, hatched in March of 1980, was plucked by the parents, as was the first. A reason for this abnormal behavior could not be found; the varied diet precludes the possibility of a deficiency. It was remarkable that the cockatoos altered their feeding habits only with the hatching of the first chick. Before, they accepted only sunflower seed and turned down all other foods; now they eat all kinds of seeds, fruit and green food, as well as cheese, hard-boiled egg, and finely ground beef heart. It is also noteworthy that so far fresh twigs offered for gnawing have never been accepted, while old dry branches or, better yet, thick wooden planks and boards enjoy a special popularity. Though not bred in 1981 becuase of a renovation, the animals are now again incubating two fertile eggs in a sturdier aviary with double wiring. Between the successful breedings, single eggs were laid repeatedly but were incubated only for a few days or not at all.

Meanwhile, breeding has been successful for many other bird fanciers here and abroad. In Switzerland alone, fourteen young had been reared by 1981, according to that country's stock list.

C. haematuropygia, male

Red-vented Cockatoo,
Cacatua haematuropygia

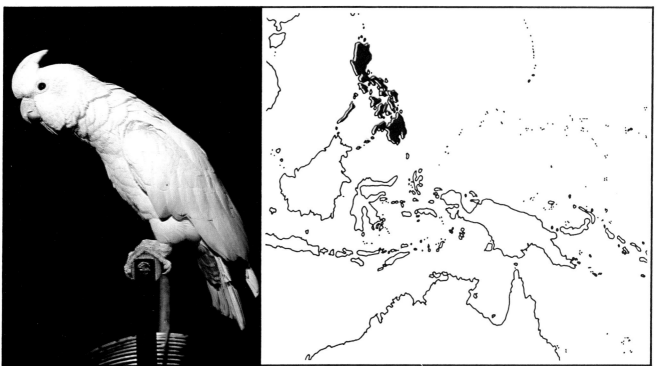

Red-vented Cockatoo
Cacatua haematuropygia
(P. L. S. Müller) 1776

German: *Rotsteisskakadu*
French: *Cacatoès de Philippines*
Dutch: *Philippijnse Kaketoe*

Characteristics: Size, about 31 cm.; mainly white with faint yellow ear patches; small, broad crest with yellowish feathers at the base; under wing coverts yellow; under tail coverts orange red with white tips; underside of the tail yellowish; naked white eye ring; beak gray white; iris dark brown in the male, red in the female. Young birds can be recognized by the salmon-colored rump; the iris is fully colored only at about three years of age.
Distribution: Philippines, including Palawan and the Sulu Islands.

Life in the Wild In its range the Red-vented Cockatoo is comparatively common wherever the original vegetation is still found. A forest dweller, this small cockatoo frequents open areas only occasionally; the expanding lumber trade in the Philippines and neighboring islands may threaten its existence. Occasionally, small groups visit rice and grain fields that lie near the edge of the forest; while larger flocks of these cockatoos often gather to feed here, as a rule they are seen only in pairs or small groups of as many as eight animals. Their flight appears buoyant; despite their great speed, the animals are very skillful. Their food consists mainly of seeds, fruits, nuts, and berries. Very little is known so far about their courtship and breeding behavior. A few nests were found between May and June. As a rule, three or four eggs are laid (averaging 38 × 27 mm.), and the young hatch after an incubation period of about twenty-four days. Both adults participate in incubation and rearing.

Keeping While the Red-vented Cockatoo used to be an absolute rarity in zoos and among bird fanciers, it has been more frequently offered for sale by importers since the mid-1970s. Initially its price was quite high, but since there is no demand for this cockatoo in the trade—as a rule, it is kept only for breeding purposes—the price soon fell to a lower level. The author has seen shipments of these animals that contained more than fifty birds. The cockatoos were usually in excellent condition, but their care presents problems, however. In recent years the author has owned more than ten of these cockatoos, attractive because of their smallness; the fate of more than twenty other animals is well known.

In good condition, acclimated without problems, the animals present hardly any difficulties during the first months. If one obtains young specimens, they become extremely tame and affectionate; housed in a roomy aviary, they are very lively and lovable animals. Heard only in the morning and evening, their voices are not particularly loud even then; the growling sounds remind one of the Gang-gang Cockatoo *(C. fimbriatum)*. Older animals usually stay shy for the rest of their lives. It is best to select younger specimens and to wait for reproductive maturity, which probably takes three or four years.

The problems in caring for these cockatoos do not start until the first major molt. Although well fed on a varied diet, the birds' feather condition constantly worsens. Wing and tail feathers are shed, and the growing feather shafts die off shortly after penetrating the skin or develop incompletely. At first the contour feathers are still immaculate, but the birds soon become unable to fly and must be put into a cage. A short time later, the first bare spots in the body plumage can be seen, and after a few months the birds are more or less naked. As their health is otherwise undisturbed, they will live for another year or two and then often die of hypothermia.

The cause of this mysterious illness is still unknown; of the fresh imports known to the author, about seventy percent eventually showed it. This illness also occurs in other cockatoo species, but much more rarely. Several animal clinics that were consulted could give no advice; increased doses of minerals were no help, nor were hormone treatments. Birds that had been kept in warm rooms were affected, as were aviary birds; it is noteworthy that females fall ill more often than males. Once they have succeeded in getting through one or two molts in captivity, there are usually no further problems, and the animals remain in good condition.

If one decides to purchase a Red-vented cockatoo, the condition of its plumage should be carefully examined. Especially with this species, one should choose very carefully, paying special attention to the complement of tail and wing feathers. It doesn't make any difference whether the animals are trimmed. If one discovers shafts with dark blood, these cockatoos can with certainty be considered lost. It is best to select birds that are in the middle of molting. If the plumage contains several healthy flight-feather shafts well supplied with red blood, one can buy with confidence. The author has never had any difficulties with such birds.

Another problem is the great pugnacity of these cockatoos. Especially when inclined to breed, the cocks become extremely aggressive and sometimes attack their hens. For the author too, attempts at pairing often took a bloody turn, and several instances in which the cock tore off his mate's entire upper mandible are known. The cause for this abnormal behavior might be the forced pairing; also, these small cockatoos appear to have greater space requirements than many other species of the genus. Trimming the cock's wings helps the situation but may reduce his ability to mate.

Feeding Because of the difficulties described, with this species special attention must be given to a well-balanced diet. In addition to the usual seed mixture—sunflower, teazle, wheat, oats, and small seeds—small nuts and berries should be given. Once the birds become accustomed to them, all kinds of fruits and vegetables—particularly dandelion leaves and roots—are eaten gladly. These should be supplemented with a multivitamin and mineral mixture. Fresh twigs for gnawing must always be available.

Breeding Probably because of the difficulties cited, reports of successful breeding are rare thus far. Even in compatible pairs, eggs are not laid despite regular mating over many years. Perhaps darkening the shelter room may help, because in the wild these forest dwellers prefer to nest where light is dim.

In 1979, three young were reared by hand in the San Diego Zoo. Hybrids between a male Red-vented Cockatoo and a female Major Mitchell's Cockatoo *(C. leadbeateri)* were reported in 1973 by a Florida zoo.

The best results so far were had by W. Eichelberger of Switzerland; by 1978, no fewer than nine had been produced. A female, owned by this fancier since 1966, was able to be paired only in 1970; at that time, Red-vented Cockatoos still were great rarities in Europe. Before pairing the cockatoo had laid repeatedly but, understandably, incubated unreliably. The following year, eggs were laid again; however, the three eggs proved to be infertile, as the tame cock, imprinted on its previous owner, paid hardly any attention to his mate.

In the same year, another four of these small cockatoos were purchased; however, one pair died shortly afterwards. The two males remaining were put in with the female. Soon the extra bird had to be removed from the aviary because he was furiously attacked by the pair which had formed. A nest box 80 cm. high was chewed apart, but a nest of heavy boards 2 m. deep was finally accepted. In the spring of 1974, the first egg was laid in the box, and from then on both animals were extremely shy and seldom visible. Unnecessary inspections and disturbances were avoided. After thirty days, a cheeping was heard for the first time; daily it became louder, indicating that both youngsters were thriving wonderfully. After a nestling period of about eight weeks, they left the box. In the following years the pair raised regularly two or three young. But things did not always go smoothly. In 1976, the pair did not want to breed; as a test, another pair was put into the aviary. Within minutes, the old breeding female paired with the new cock, and both chased the other birds so furiously that they had to be removed at once. Six days later, the first egg was in the box, and incubation and rearing proceeded normally. Unfortunately, one day in 1977, the breeding cock was found dead on the floor. The female was extremely choosey with the change of mates; only the third cock was accepted. Together, they reared two young. The loss of another animal unfortunately ended this proud series of successes.

Goffin's Cockatoo
Cacatua goffini
(Finsch) 1863

German: *Goffin's Kakadu*
French: *Cacatoès de Goffin*
Dutch: *Goffins Kaketoe*

Characteristics: Size, about 29 cm.; white, with pink-colored lores; small round crest; pink tinge on head feathers; undersides of wing and tail feathers yellowish; naked blue white eye ring; beak whitish; feet light gray; iris black in the male, red in the female.
Distribution: Tanimbar Islands.

Life in the Wild   There are few reports from observations in the wild. The species is said to be common on the larger of the eighty-five Tanimbar Islands, such as Yamdena, Fordate, and Selaru, in the extensive forests. As typical forest

C. goffini, female

Goffin's Cockatoo,
Cacatua goffini

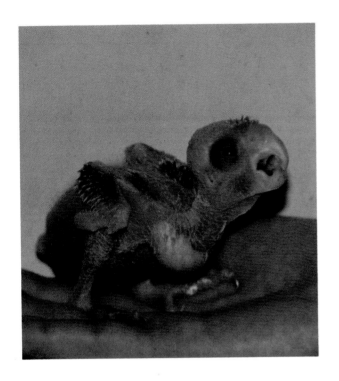

Goffin's Cockatoo (*C. goffini*) in the course of hand-rearing: 13 days old, 29.5 grams (above, left); 25 days, 78 grams (above, right); and 43 days, 222 grams (right).

dwellers, however, they are increasingly threatened by agricultural expansion. In 1970, the deforestation planned for the island group began; sooner or later, only strict protection of the biotope will help to preserve these cockatoos.

According to reports by Dr. Strunden of Essen, they have no fixed breeding period, but breed throughout the year. As a rule, two to three eggs are laid and incubated by both parents. They are reported to occasionally cause some damage in the natives' corn fields; however, they are not being persecuted for this.

Keeping Because of their plainness, these cockatoos are usually kept in aviaries, rarely as cage birds. Only young specimens will become tame and affectionate; keeping them for breeding purposes suits this species especially. For many years, this small cockatoo was seldom available. Only since 1970 has it been traded regularly, yet never in large numbers. Initially, these birds were not recognized as this species but were often offered for sale as Little Corellas; the pair kept by the author was purchased under that name.

The regular importation during recent years can be explained by the deforestation program in their range. After the hordes of woodcutters pass through, who nowadays do not cut single hardwood trees but systematically clear acre after acre and leave only the bare ground, the errant birds are captured and sent overseas. Even with the strictest import regulations, the animals can hardly be saved without protecting the biotope. The Goffin's Cockatoos available here usually come from biotopes no longer intact, as capture and transport are too expensive in the rainforest. Because of the low demand, the prices paid for this cockatoo nowadays are no longer high. Nevertheless, it seems important that more bird fanciers take an interest in these little fellows, especially since imports have declined again in the last three years. Whether this is caused by decimation of the wild population or is a result of the low demand cannot be determined.

Kept in the aviary, Goffin's Cockatoo is easy to care for. If, during the construction of the aviary, its strong need to gnaw and its natural living conditions are considered—the animals should have an opportunity of finding shady, well-hidden areas in the aviary—they usually stay in good condition for a long time and hold up well in our climate. A temperate shelter room must be available, however. That many animals are quite loud should also be taken into consideration in their accommodations.

Feeding Sunflower seed, teazle, and domestic grains (also sprouted). Fresh corn and fruit are taken gladly. Insect larvae and hard cheese cut into small pieces will enrich the menu.

Breeding This cockatoo has been bred repeatedly in Western Europe during the last few years. The first success was had by E. G. B. Schulte of Holland, in 1974. A recently acquired pair, housed in a roomy cage, laid three eggs in the nest box (25 × 25 × 40 cm.) beginning on June 15. In the middle of December, two young birds from a second clutch left the nest. In the following year, the animals came into breeding condition in May; again two young were reared. Breedings in several neighboring European countries followed. In Switzerland, the first young were reared in 1979; thus far, three breeders have been successful there.

Breeding in Germany probably succeeded first for T. Weise of Dortmund. His observations coincide with those made by Rosemary Low, whose pair proceeded to breed successfully for the first time in 1979, after seven years in her collection. The young that hatched after an incubation period of twenty-eight days were fed for only a short time, however, and then had to be reared by hand. Weise first saw birds of this species in October 1972 at a bird show in Switzerland. In the same year, some importers in Germany first offered Goffin's Cockatoos for sale. At that time, the birds were still quite expensive (DM 1200. each).

This bird lover also discovered his first "pair" at a bird show. The animals were not shy and attracted attention by copulating several times a day in the show aviary. Since they had gnawed through all of the owner's wooden aviaries, they were for sale. For lack of space, the animals were kept in a low, comparatively dark attic aviary (2.7 × 0.8 × 0.8 m.); several nest boxes were offered. Although the birds were compatible and continued to mate regularly, they made no other preparations for breeding. Therefore, the iris color of the cockatoos was checked in the light of a bright lamp; it was equally dark in both animals, showing they were both cocks. A little later, a female was purchased. She could be recognized by smaller stature and a brown iris ring. When she was put into the aviary with the two males, one cock had to be removed after five minutes because the other was chasing it furiously.

In December of the same year, the pair proceeded to breed; however, the only youngster was thrown into the water dish by the parents immediately after hatching. One year later, in February 1978, a second young bird was bred, which turned out to be rather weak. After four months it left the nest. Since it was no longer being fed by the parents, it had to be helped along by hand; today, it is very tame. On August 22, 1978, after an incubation period of twenty-eight days, a third cockatoo hatched. It was reared without complications, and it left the nest log on November 25, 1978. Only hollow logs standing on the ground were accepted as nesting sites; they were chewed so badly that they had to be replaced after every breeding. First, all the bark was gnawed off the trunk, then the remaining wood was thoroughly polished. The same behavior has already been described in detail for the Galah (*E. roseicapillus)*. After relocating in 1979, the pair could be housed in a bright, spacious aviary; although all kinds of nesting sites have been offered, the animals have failed to make any attempt to breed.

Little Corella
Cacatua sanguinea
Gould 1842

German: *Nacktaugenkakadu, Rotzügelkakadu*
French: *Cacatoès à lunettes rouges*
Dutch: *Roodteugelkaketoe*

Two subspecies No species gives more headaches to the systematists than this one. Many authors treat Goffin's Cockatoo (*C. goffini)* as a subspecies of *sanguinea;* however, this thesis in no longer tenable. Difficulties also arise in clarifying the relationship between the Little Corella and the Long-billed Corella (*C. tenuirostris);* repeatedly the two have been merged under one specific name or the other. While Forshaw (1973) in *Parrots of the World* treats them as separate species, in *Australian Parrots,* 2nd edition, he gives specific rank only to the nominate form of the Long-billed Corella (*tenuirostris).* The subspecies *pastinator,* based on investigations of the morphology of the beak and crest and body size, is placed with the Little Corella, which is called by the prior name, *pastinator.* The parrot known here as Little Corella is thus given the rank of a subspecies: *C. pastinator sanguinea.*

The morphological characters mentioned are especially subject to evolutionary change. The development of the size and shape of the beak depends on feeding habits. Such an adaptation to the same function in the course of phylogeny is convergent evolution and by itself does not make a valid statement about ancestral relationships. In such cases all other aspects, such as behavior, hybridization in the wild, etc., must be considered. Since in the author's opinion this matter has not been clarified sufficiently, the taxonomy originally chosen by Forshaw (1969, 1973) is allowed to stand, though there is no doubt that there is a very close relationship between the two species.

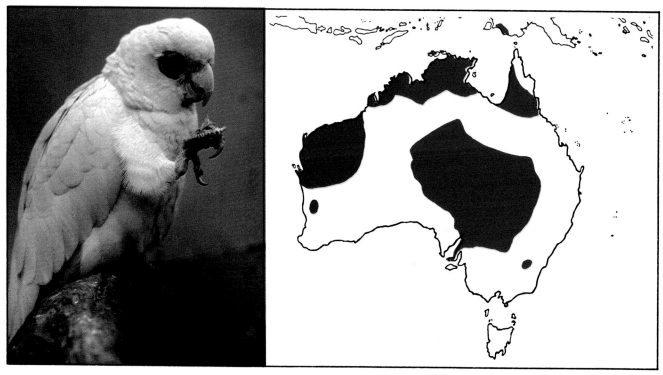

C. s. sanguinea, male

Little Corella,
Cacatua sanguinea

1. *C. sanguinea sanguinea* Gould

Characteristics: Size, about 38 cm.; plumage white with salmon-colored feathers on lores, crown, cheeks, and throat; small round crest; gray blue naked eye ring which extends considerably below the eye; beak light; feet gray; iris brown in both sexes. Females are smaller and may be recognized by the less extensive eye ring.

Distribution: Eastern, northwestern, and northern Australia, with the exception of the Cape York Peninsula.

2. *C. s. normantoni* (Mathews)

Characteristics: Like the nominate form, but somewhat smaller, and usually a weaker pink color in the plumage.

Distribution: Southern New Guinea; coastal regions of the Cape York Peninsula and the Gulf of Carpentaria in northern Queensland.

Life in the Wild The Little Corella was probably the first Australian parrot observed and described by a European. Nowadays too, the species is an everyday sight in its range. Observations show that these cockatoos have continued to multiply and, because of the pressure of intraspecific competition, spread more and more widely. Like the Galah *(E. roseicapillus),* they profit from the advancing cultivation, because agriculture provides new food sources and waterholes. They are loud, conspicuous birds, and they are usually seen in flocks that may number thousands of birds by the end of the breeding season. A flock sighted near Wyndham in Western Australia was estimated to contain sixty to seventy thousand animals. Proportionately great damage is done by these cockatoos to agriculture; for this reason, they are not protected in most areas.

Little Corellas are nomadic, especially during the dry season, always searching for food and water. Early travelers to Australia understood their habits: the cockatoos usually stay near watering places, and the pioneers often followed the flock returning at dusk. The animals are usually found along watercourses in the open country covered with trees and shrubs. Although they usually find their food—mainly grass seeds, herbaceous plants, roots, and berries—in the open steppes on the ground, they like to spend the hot midday hours in the branches of *Eucalyptus* trees, where they occasionally search for wood-boring insect larvae. Even though the species has been observed in the mangrove swamps of the Cape York Peninsula, they seem to avoid dense forests, as a rule. Very early in the morning, the animals fly to

waterholes to drink. The approach of the flock can be heard from afar, although this species is no match for the Sulphur-crested Cockatoo *(C. galerita)* as far as noise is concerned. Nor can a group foraging for food in the early morning or late afternoon be missed. Extremely shy, they will take wing at the slightest disturbance, shrieking loudly.

As inhabitants of the dry interior regions, they apparently have no fixed breeding season; instead, this depends on climatic conditions. If conditions are favorable, two to three broods

Waterhole in the flood plain east of Darwin. Pandanus trees growing directly on the banks are surrounded with eucalyptus savannah. Little Corellas (C. s. sanguinea), Sulphur-crested (C. g. galerita), and Red-tailed (C. m. macrorhynchus) cockatoos are regularly observed here.

are often reared one after the other. Thus nests have been found in almost all seasons, with the exception of the dry months around the turn of the year. They prefer to nest in hollow *Eucalyptus* trees near watercourses, but rock crevices and termite mounds also serve as breeding sites. There are no woodpeckers in Australia, and breeding cavities excavated mainly by termites are rare. The three to four eggs (averaging 37.0 × 27.5 mm.) are laid at two-day intervals and incubated for twenty-one days by both parents. After a relatively short growth period of forty-five to fifty days, the young fledge.

Keeping   Although abundant in their range, Little Corellas have never come to Europe in great numbers. In Australia, they are frequently kept as house pets and, if obtained young, are said to become affectionate and tame. They also have good talent for mimicry, but their loud voices often gets on the keeper's nerves before long. Elsewhere they are usually kept in pairs for breeding purposes. In the late seventies, the species suddenly was offered in large numbers and at good prices. Although the name "Australian Bare-eyed Cockatoo" was designed to increase the demand, the birds in question were, almost without exception, the New Guinea subspecies. The prices were too low to make smuggling from Australia worthwhile. Only few bird fanciers keep this cockatoo, and so it is probably no longer imported because of the low demand.

If well acclimated, they may be wintered without heat. They are undemanding and will breed comparatively easily if kept in an aviary. The small number of reports can be explained by the low numbers imported in former years. Lacking mates, they have been crossed with the Galah *(E. roseicapillus);* hybrids of the two species have also been observed in the wild. The aviary must be constructed of metal, since Little Corellas are great chewers. In selecting its location, their loud voices should be kept in mind, for they use them especially when approached by strangers.

Feeding   Sunflower seed, oats, and wheat in sprouted form are preferably eaten off the ground. Especially during breeding, the seeds should be raked into the ground slightly (beware of worm infestations!). Apples, carrots, spinach, and mangel are enjoyed; nuts, berries, and small seeds should also be given.

Breeding   The first breeding success dates back to the year 1907 in London; in Italy the first young were reared in 1923, in Holland in 1926. The reports that only females incubate are certainly based on faulty observation. The greatest success was at the San Diego Zoo, where one pair alone raised 103 young between 1929 and 1970; the majority were reared by hand, however. Further breeding successes were achieved by breeders here and abroad. In light of the small extent to which these birds were kept, such success permits the conclusion that this species is easily bred.

The most success in Germany was had by A. Preussiger of Neuwied during the seventies. His pair, housed in a spacious outdoor flight with an attached shelter room, bred in a 50 l. barrel situated in the shelter room. Although fertile, no young hatched from the eggs, which were incubated by both parents. The pair had the habit of throwing out all the nesting material put into the breeding cavity. Failure occurred not for lack of humidity—which is not high naturally for these inhabitants of the dry interior—but because the eggs were constantly rolling around on the concave floor of the barrel. A nest shape made of concrete remedied this, and from the next clutch in 1976, two young hatched after an incubation period of twenty-one days.

Covered with a thin layer of yellow down, they stretched their heads and necks during every nest inspection and begged for food. At fifteen days, the eyes were open; the young looked like small hedgehogs, for their heads, backs, and wings were covered with feather shafts breaking through the skin. Nest inspection no longer provoked begging movements;

instead the nestlings hissed and made the rocking threat movements typical of cockatoos. At the age of twenty-three days, the entire body was covered by light feather shafts, and by thirty-five days, they were almost completely feathered. The young left the nest forty-five days after hatching, but continued to be fed by the parents for a few weeks more. Even six weeks later they occasionally begged for food. After this initial success, the pair regularly reared two young every year. Another German breeder, W. Heinrich of Mainz, reports a nestling period of fifty days.

Long-billed Corella
Cacatua tenuirostris
(Kuhl) 1820

German: *Nasenkakadu*
French: *Cacatoès nasique*
Dutch: *Neuskaketoe*

Two subspecies Two subspecies with separate ranges can be distinguished with certainty by the coloration of the plumage.

1. *C. tenuirostris tenuirostris* (Kuhl)
Characteristics: Size, 38 cm.; plumage white; forehead, lores, band across throat, and bases of the feathers of the head, neck, and upper breast bright orange red; undersides of tail and wing feathers yellow; small, closely held round crest; naked blue gray eye ring; beak horn-colored with markedly elongated upper mandible; legs and feet gray; iris dark brown; females can be distinguished only by the smaller head and beak.
Distribution: Southeastern Australia.

2. *C. t. pastinator* (Gould)
Characteristics: Larger than the nominate form; orange red neck band is absent; nape and upper breast pure white.
Distribution: Southwestern Australia.

Life in the Wild Already in 1969 Forshaw pointed out that this species is becoming increasingly rare. In place of the large flocks of some decades ago, the animals today are seen roaming about in pairs or small groups. It is probable that the early European settlements and land clearing led to the decline of the species. Pressed by the more adaptable Little Corella *(C. sanguinea)*, they retreated further and further into unsettled arid regions. In many areas they have completely disappeared. Once hunted for damaging crops, today the Long-billed Corella is fully protected.

Long-billed Corellas are loud birds that are often heard before they are sighted. In small groups of two to eight birds usually, they forage on the ground. By means of the long upper mandible, they dig for succulent roots, tubers, and bulbs. Thus they at least partly avoid competition with other cockatoos inhabiting the dry regions. However, grass seeds, herbaceous plants, nuts, and fruit are also components of their diet. If disturbed, they take wing with loud shrieking; during flight they make peculiar-sounding two-syllable contact calls that serve to keep the group together. The Long-billed Corella prefers wooded grassland and savannalike woodland. Its nests are usually found in tall *Eucalyptus* trees near watercourses or waterholes. The breeding season falls between August and November. As a rule, the clutch consists of two or three eggs (averaging 33.2 × 25.1 mm.). Careful field observations of its breeding biology are not available; more accurate research would be desirable for the preservation of the species.

Keeping Long-billed Corellas nowadays are rarely found in the hands of bird fanciers; seldom imported, they are found in only a few collections. In the last century, however, they were available more frequently and often kept as tame pets.

Assessments of their temperament differ widely. While Gould and Brehm consider them not particularly attractive as pets, Finsch describes

C. t. tenuirostris

Long-billed Corella,
Cacatua tenuirostris

them as remarkably lovable. This probably depends very much on the age at which the birds were captured. M. Meissner of Stuttgart had a pair that always remained shy. Dr. Burkard of Switzerland describes his pair as extremely lovable, friendly birds that never entirely lost their shyness toward humans. Forshaw describes birds of this species as the best talkers among the cockatoos. But it seems idle to discuss such characteristics further; anyway, because of their rarity they should only be kept for breeding purposes. Single caged birds should be put together in cooperative breeding programs.

Since they are extremely quarrelsome they are hardly suited to being kept in a mixed collection. In planning the aviary, their behavior should be taken into account. Only a strongly constructed aviary will withstand their strong beaks; the floor of the aviary should not be con-

crete, since the animals spend the greater part of the day on the ground. In 1976, the author was able to observe a pair in the Neuwied Zoo digging large holes and almost completely disappearing in them. Of course the aviary must be enclosed in such a way that the animals will not escape through the tunnels they dig. If the birds are not given the opportunity for using their long beaks in the manner already mentioned, these will soon become unnaturally long or deformed. Kept in a fashion suited to the species, the birds usually do quite well in captivity and are not sensitive to our weather. Nevertheless, a temperate shelter room must be available in order not to miss a possible winter breeding.

Feeding A basic seed mixture of equal parts of sunflower seed, wheat, and cracked corn;

142

millet, canary seed, and oats will be taken. Peanuts, almonds, and fruit – particularly grapes, cherries, and oranges – are said to be eaten gladly. Freshly planted grass sod and roots are welcome.

Breeding The first documented aviary breeding probably took place in the San Diego Zoo. A pair that came to the zoo in 1951 began to breed eight years later in a nest box set 4 m. above the floor of the aviary. All other nesting sites that had been offered through the years had been ignored. In order to stimulate laying, the keeper additionally fed mealworms and slugs. The single egg was incubated for twenty-nine days. After a nestling period of ten weeks, the youngster was seen for the first time outside the box, and three weeks later reports say it was foraging on the ground by itself. The pair was successful also in following years.

The Australian first breeding belongs to Alan Lendon. In 1968, his pair bred in a hollow log in the shelter room of the aviary. Three eggs were laid at two-day intervals at the end of September; both birds took turns at incubation, reported as twenty-four days. One young bird left the nest at the age of seven weeks. Meanwhile, there have been breeding successes in Tasmania and New Zealand.

So far, it seems no breeding has occurred in Europe. While a few bird fanciers in Germany keep this species, nothing more than egg laying has taken place. According to oral reports, Long-billed Corellas are not easy to pair; the cocks especially are aggressive. It is hoped that a breeding stock of these interesting cockatoos can be established in order to guarantee the survival of this species at least in captivity and also to supplement the wild population by animals bred in aviaries.

C. ducorpsii, female

Ducorps's Cockatoo,
Cacatua ducorpsii

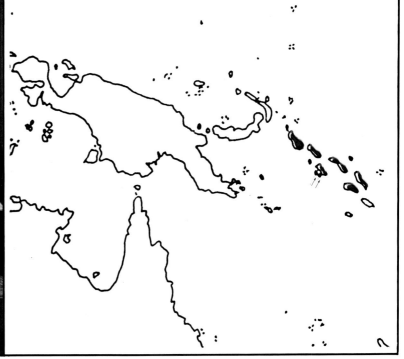

Ducorps's Cockatoo
Cacatua ducorpsii
Pucheran 1850

German: *Salomonenkakadu*
French: *Cacatoès de Ducorps*
Dutch: *Ducorps Kaketoe*

Characteristics: Size, about 31 cm.; pure white plumage; only under wing and under tail feathers slightly yellowish; round crest broader and longer than Goffin's Cockatoo; white blue naked eye ring; beak and feet gray white; iris brown to black in the male, reddish in the female.
Distribution: Solomon Islands from Bougainville to Malaita; absent from the San Cristobal Islands.

Life in the Wild In their range Ducorps's Cockatoos can be seen daily. On the various islands, they live primarily in lowland forests, but they are also found up to altitudes of 1700 m. H. Leibfarth of Vaihingen observed them many times in September 1979 on Guadalcanal and Malaita, where the species is said to be especially common. The animals usually appear in pairs, but small groups of up to eight animals were also observed. Every evening they congregate on sleeping trees near human habitation to spend the night. In the early morning hours the loud calls of the cockatoos can be heard again. Attracted by corn and grain fields, they follow man into the towns and also cause considerable damage to fruit orchards. In the fields, they dig for sweet potatoes. Nevertheless, the cockatoos are not hunted in their homeland, but young animals discovered when a breeding tree is cut down are hand-reared by the natives and kept as tame pets. They seem to retreat to less accessible forest regions to breed, for there are no reports on the breeding biology of this species.

Keeping Ducorps's Cockatoos are seldom imported; for this reason alone, they should be kept in pairs in an aviary, and single animals must be paired in cooperative breeding programs. Export from the Solomons, independent since 1977, is very difficult; the same was true during previous years, when the islands were still under Australian control. In the U.S.A., the species has been kept occasionally; well-acclimated birds are no more problematical than other members of the genus. In 1976, Bregulla brought a few pairs to Europe; the animals were acclimated in the aviaries of Dr. Burkard in Switzerland and then some were resold. According to the Swiss stock list, today few bird fanciers have this species.

Feeding Sunflower seed, teazle, wheat, oats, and millet. Cooked corn, fruit, and carrots are enjoyed.

Breeding Thus far there are no reports of a successful breeding. Eggs were laid repeatedly for two Swiss bird fanciers, but the clutches were either infertile or were not incubated. In two instances of young animals hatching—the incubation period is said to last twenty-eight days—they were killed on the first day by the parents. In any case, Ducorps's Cockatoo seems to be as aggressive as the Red-vented Cockatoo (*C. haematuropygia*). According to oral reports from their keepers, the animals can be paired only with great difficulty and are extremely aggressive, especially when in the mood to breed. Attacking cocks frequently injure their mates. Because of their great rarity, it must be hoped that this species will soon be bred and thereby be found in our aviaries.

Genus *NYMPHICUS*
Wagler 1832

One species.

Cockatiel
Nymphicus hollandicus
(Kerr) 1792

German: *Nymphensittich*
French: *Perruche calopsite*
Dutch: *Valkparkiet*

Characteristics (wild-colored form): Size, about 32 cm.; main color of plumage gray, underside of body sometimes mixed with brown; forehead, crest, forecrown, cheeks and throat bright yellow in the male; ear patch bright orange, greater wing coverts and distal secondaries white; upper tail coverts and central tail feathers pale gray, outer tail feathers and underside of the tail dark gray to black; beak and legs dark gray; cere feathered; iris dark brown. Crown, crest, and cheeks of the female only faintly yellow, mixed with gray; rump, lower back, and central tail feathers pale gray; the outer tail feathers yellow irregularly marbled with dark gray. On the inner vanes of the wing flights, females have numerous white spots. Young birds resemble adult females in their plumage, but the beak is flesh-colored at first and turns dark only at about three months of age. Young males already have more yellow feathers on their heads; the outer tail feathers are more faintly marbled than those of young females, and the spots on the inner vanes of the wing flights are also less pronounced.
Distribution: The whole Australian continent, with the exception of the humid coastal regions in the north, east, and south.

Life in the Wild Like many inhabitants of the arid regions of central Australia with its very irregular precipitation, *N. hollandicus* also has an extremely nomadic way of life. Its occurrence is determined by changes in food availability. Usually pairs or small groups are seen on the ground, where they find grass seeds. Large flocks are found especially during seasonal migrations. In dry spells they will suddenly leave areas in which they were frequently seen previously, and reappear in large flocks in other areas. As a nomadic species, they are good colonizers. The appearance of a flock (sedentary species usually occur singly in strange areas) makes the establishment of new populations possible in previously unsettled areas. Since natural barriers are absent from their range, the different populations mix constantly, preventing the formation of subspecies, so common in the genus *Platycercus* (rosellas). With the exception of dense forests, Cockatiels are found in almost every habitat. Besides high trees along rivers, they are found in open savannas, in the low mulga scrub steppes, and even in the desertlike spinifex grassland.

Outside of the breeding season, this cockatoo wanders about in small flocks of about fifty animals. In the dry season, aggregations of more than a thousand individuals can be seen near waterholes, and even in these situations firmly paired animals stay close together the year around. One element promoting flock cohesion is the white wing coverts. Whether in a male, a female, or a juvenile animal, they serve during flight as a signal directed to the flock. In addition, the flock call is heard continuously during flight. The flight of *N. hollandicus* is swift and direct. Neither the undulations of the *Platycercus* species nor the rapid turns of those of the genera *Polytelis* ("splendid parakeets") and *Neophema* (grass-parakeets) are seen; instead it goes forward in a straight line.

The habits of nomadism and flocking profoundly affect behavior. Group behavior dominates over individual behavior, for this alone guarantees the integrity of the flock. Through a transfer of mood, all the animals follow the same daily rhythm; they all eat, rest, or preen at about the same time. Cockatiels like to sit on dead branches, where their gray plumage blends so closely with the color of the branches that they are difficult to see, especially since they usually position their bodies along the direction of the branch. Here they are less shy than when on the ground; since they cannot scan the area as easily from there, like most inhabitants of the savanna, they seek safety in flight. When drinking, they usually approach the watering place flying fast, circle a long time, and then drop almost vertically to the ground. They never land on the bank, but directly in the shallow water, where they quickly drink a few swallows, then hurriedly rush away.

The breeding season of *N. hollandicus* depends on climatic conditions, precipitation above all. If the conditions are favorable, several broods often follow one another. Generally, the breeding season may be noted as lasting from August to December, but nests with young can also be found in April. Cockatiels breed in knotholes; they prefer dead trees from which they can survey the area. Of some interest is the distribution of nesting sites

and the extent to which another pair of the same species near the breeding site is tolerated. This behavior contrasts with other social behaviors. Unlike some other cockatoos *(C. sanguinea* and *E. roseicapillus),* cockatiels never nest several to one tree or nearby.

Keeping Already in 1788, *Nymphicus hollandicus* was described and named by Gmelin* in his *Systema naturae.* The first reports about its life and distribution in the wild were published by J. Gould in 1840. In 1846, an attempt was made to breed them in the Jardin des Plantes in Paris; with what result is no longer known. Today, the Cockatiel is considered fully domesticated and, next to the Budgerigar *(Melopsittacus undulatus),* is the member of the order Psittaciformes most frequently kept in captivity. It is often found as a tame pet in a cage, as well as in breeders' aviaries. Nowadays breeding is successful very often.

* His name, *Psittacus novaehollandiae,* was preoccupied and replaced by Kerr's *P. hollandicus.*

N. hollandicus, pair

**Cockatiel,
*Nymphicus hollandicus***

Acacia and eucalyptus trees in the valleys of the Macdonnell Ranges in central Australia, which are more fertile than the surrounding desert areas. Here one finds mostly Galahs (*E. r. roseicapillus*), Red-tailed Cockatoos (*C. m. samueli*), and Cockatiels (*N. hollandicus*).

If a young animal is purchased directly from the breeder, it will, as a rule, quickly become tame and affectionate toward its keeper. Naturally, in temperament the Cockatiel cannot be compared with any other cockatoo, but this species is particularly suitable for beginners. Moreover, no further reference to wild populations need be made here. Young males quickly learn to imitate a few words and to whistle short melodies. Since their voice is not loud, they are suitable for being kept in close quarters. Some animals, however, use their voices extensively and at great length, and even the most melodic-sounding notes can become annoying. Tame birds especially should be regularly allowed to fly free in the house; kept in a spacious cage, they then will readily go on to breed. In an outdoor aviary, they are congenial and extremely hardy in our climate. A shelter room must be available, but this need not be heated. Since they are not great chewers, a wooden structure with thin wire mesh is completely sufficient. As they are extremely peaceable, several pairs can be kept in large aviaries. They can be housed with Budgerigars *(M. undulatus)* as well.

Feeding A seed mixture containing a high proportion of millet and canary seed. Greens, fruit, or sprouts are often taken only after a long familiarization period.

Breeding Around 1850, the Cockatiel was first bred in Germany; today, breeding it is commonplace and does not present the bird fancier with any great problems. They will breed as readily in a roomy cage as in an aviary; for nesting, a simple box made of hardboard is sufficient (20 × 20 × 35 cm.). Reports of new color varieties are published steadily; those interested are referred to the relevant literature.

In early spring, or almost any season in heated rooms, the courtship display of the male can be observed. With slightly raised wings, he trips back and forth on the perch, only stepping sideways. He continually moves toward the female and away again. Three to five sideways steps in the direction of the female are always followed by a similar number in the opposite direction. Characteristic of *Nymphicus* is the courtship song, which is delivered either before, but usually during, the sidestepping. Short monosyllabic notes are linked together to form a melodic phrase. In many color varieties, this courtship song can be used to determine sex, since sexual dimorphism is often absent. In the literature, courtship flights with sudden turns are described. After landing, the males will remain sitting on the branch for a while with open wings and fanned tail; often they will also hang head-downward from the perch.

When Cockatiels are ready to breed, about three weeks before the eggs are laid, copulation occurs irregularly, usually only once a day. The early morning hours are somewhat favored, but it can take place at any other time of day. The readiness to mate increases and reaches its climax shortly before egg laying begins. Five or six copulations irregularly throughout the day, often with only an hour's interval, are the rule. At the same time, courtship activity becomes less frequent. After the first egg is laid, the number of copulations decreases quickly.

With Cockatiels, the choice of a nesting site is always made by the male. Several weeks before egg laying, he begins to inspect the available nest boxes, approaching the entrances with caution at first. A precipitous entrance is probably countered by an inborn fear, because tree hollows are often the hiding places of enemies of cavity breeders. This fear and the resultant tendency to flee are evident in the animal's behavior. This has sufficiently abated after a few days so that the male will enter. As a rule, eggs are laid at intervals of two days; occasionally, the next egg is laid in thirty-six hours.

The average clutch consists of four or five eggs (averaging 24.5 × 19.0 mm.), but seven or eight are not rare. Whether this is a consequence of domestication cannot be determined. From the second egg on, but sometimes from the third, the clutch is tightly incubated by both adults. As a rule, the male incubates from 6 AM to 2 PM, the female the rest of the time. The average incubation period for *N. hollandicus* lasts eighteen days, not, as often stated in the literature, twenty-one days. The young hatch at intervals, but these do not correspond exactly to the two-day laying intervals, since the animals begin incubation only when the clutch is half complete. The first two young usually hatch within twelve hours, the others during the next two or three days. Thus, the differences in development among them is not so great that the older ones push away their younger siblings at feeding time. In addition, all the siblings are fledged at about the same time and leave the breeding cavity almost together at about thirty-three days of age.

A few minutes after hatching, the young, usually not yet quite dry, are fed by the parents. They are recognized as being the right species by inherited characteristics which will be described below. Both parents feed the newly hatched young every thirty minutes or so at first. They enclose the beak of the young bird with their own, pull the head and neck upward slightly, and then execute rapid, jerky, shaking movements of the head. The head and neck of the young are moved rhythmically up and down, and they make peeping noises in the same rhythm, about two or three per second. Meanwhile they spread their wings, and fluttering can be seen during the first days of life. The peeping and the fluttering are important responses of the young. Characteristic for all cockatoos, they guarantee that rearing proceeds smoothly. After fledging, the young continue to be fed by the parents for about three more weeks. They beg actively by crouching down and, laying the crest back, swinging the head forward and backward, meanwhile rattling loudly and distinctly. During all of this, the body is usually aligned along the perch. As in the nest, the adult encloses the beak of the youngster in its own and makes the usual shaking movements of the head. The young flutter their wings furiously; the characteristic rhythmic feeding noises can also be heard.

In order to give the inexperienced breeder some clues along the way, an accurate description of the physical development of the young follows:

• *Day 1:* At hatching, young Cockatiels have yellow down. The entire body, with the exception of the belly and a circular spot on the head, is covered with it. It is noteworthy that the down of white Cockatiels is less dense than that of wild-colored ones. Young cockatoos, like young Cockatiels and broad-tailed parakeets (Platycercinae), have a primary down different in color and markings.
• *Day 7:* Dark feather shafts are visible under the skin of the wings.
• *Day 9:* The feather shafts of the wing feathers break through the skin. The shafts of the crown feathers are darkly visible under the skin. The flesh-colored feet gradually become darker, and the eyes begin to open.
• *Day 10:* The eyes are open; the feather shafts of the tail feathers break through.
• *Day 11:* The egg tooth falls off between the eleventh and fourteenth days. The feet are dark gray, the claws turn dark. The feather shafts of the crest feathers break through.

• *Day 12:* The first feather shafts on the head and body break through the skin. At their tips, they push the natal down ahead of them. In contrast to the broad-tailed parakeets, no thick, second down appears. As with cockatoos, the few "fur" downs first appear much later.
• *Day 15:* The first feather shafts on the sides of the body burst. The feather shafts on the cheeks break through.
• *Day 16:* The feather shafts of the tail and wing feathers burst.
• *Day 18:* The feather shafts of the belly feathers burst. The orange-colored cheek patches can be recognized.
• *Day 19:* The feathers of the white wing patch are completely open; it is fully feathered.
• *Day 23:* The primary down that was on the tips of the shafts of the body feathers have completely fallen off. All feather shafts have burst at their tips.
• *Day 24:* The shafts of the powder downs on the right and left flanks break through. They are white and do not push any primary down ahead of them. The few secondary "fur" downs appear.
• *Day 25:* The young are fully feathered, except for a few areas of the body, the cheek spots, the belly, and the occiput. Only the bases of the wing and tail feathers remain in their shafts.
• *Day 48:* The grown feathers are completely horny.
• *About Day 80:* The previously flesh-colored beak slowly turns dark. The final color of the beak is attained after the first complete molt, which begins at three to four months and is completed after eight to ten months. The males change into adult plumage at this time.

Systematic Position It was precisely the external shape that induced older authors such as Gould, Russ, and Brehm to put the Cockatiel with the cockatoos. The crest, the orange-colored cheek patches, and the feathered cere are immediately conspicuous characteristics.

Examinations of the morphology of the skull (Thompson) showed similarities as well as differences between the broad-tailed parakeets and the cockatoos. Since in this respect *N. hollandicus* is intermediate between the two groups, it is not feasible to base its systematic placement only on these facts, precisely because such characteristics can be considered secondary adaptations. Brereton, who puts the Cockatiel near the king parakeets *(Alisterus)* on the basis of such morphological facts, in his proof overlooks important somatic characters that are common to the cockatoos as well as the Cockatiel. He describes powder downs only in the species *C. sulfurea, C. magnificus,* and *Nymphicus,* but they also occur in all of the Cacatuinae described here, but not, however, in *Platycercus* and *Alisterus.* The beak of *N. hollandicus* differs in shape (the lower mandible is wider than the upper) from that of the broad-tailed parakeets. Just like many cockatoos, young Cockatiels leave the nest box with a flesh-colored beak that turns dark only in the course of months. The correspondence in sexual dimorphism between *Nymphicus* and the black

Pair of Cockatiels (*N. hollandicus*). During the midday heat, the animals like to rest on dead trees or telephone wires.

Cockatiels (*N. hollandicus*) occupied in social grooming.

cockatoos was described by Lendon in 1951. The structural color blue is absent from the plumage of the cockatiel and the cockatoos, but not from the broad-tailed parakeets.

Observations of the behavior of Cockatiels are written up in the literature only by Kolar, and only he points out the importance of an examination of instinctive movements and the systematic placement this would suggest for *Nymphicus.* Other authors either disregard this completely or make false and superficial statements. Berndt and Meise place the Cockatiel with the broad-tailed parakeets for the reason that its behavior is more similar to theirs

150

Cockatiel (*N. hollandicus*), male.

than to that of the cockatoos, but this is not supported by any particulars. The statement that Cockatiels do not bring food to the beak with the foot is wrong. Boetticher writes that *Nymphicus* is not related to cockatoos in any way but wisely forgoes any proof of this assertion. The observation of only such important sustentative activities as eating and drinking establishes some correspondences between *Nymphicus* and the Cacatuinae.

In the realm of social behavior the relationship between the Cockatiel and cockatoos becomes even more evident. The following discusses some behavior patterns in which the parallelism cannot be accidental. First, social grooming and mate feeding must be listed, and both must be viewed in connection with breeding behavior. Male Cockatiels, like many cockatoos, participate actively in incubation. The original significance of mate feeding, the care of the incubating female in the nest, is lost here. In contrast to the broad-tailed parakeets, which have carried mate feeding over into their courtship, it is completely absent in *Nymphicus* and in those cockatoos where both sexes incubate. Physical contact is maintained by social grooming, which can be observed in both groups even outside the breeding period.

The correspondences among significant components in the area of agonistic behavior is mentioned by Kolar. During intimidation, both Cockatiels and cockatoos spread their wings completely or partially, flap their wings, and spread their tails. These behaviors cannot be observed in the broad-tailed parakeets, in which lifting the bends of the wings and shaking the tail are the typical components of intimidation. The elements of threat behavior also correspond extensively. The animals spread their wings, sway from side to side, and make hissing, rattling sounds. Beak clapping occurs in both groups, and the threat behavior of breeding animals is completely similar. Broad-tailed parakeets do not threaten in this way.

In the area of reproductive behavior too, correspondences between the Cockatiel and cockatoos are evident. Copulating noises from the female are heard in *Nymphicus* and several cockatoos, but not in members of the Platycercinae (broad-tailed parakeets). The participation of males in incubation in *Nymphicus* and most cockatoos has been pointed out repeatedly. The manner of rearing young is so similar in both instances that it cannot be considered a coincidence. The parents use the feeding technique previously described and the young respond with rhythmic peeping and wing fluttering. Such releasers that stimulate the adult birds are completely lacking in the broad-tailed parakeets.

The behavior patterns recapitulated here and the morphological similarities demonstrate that systematic classification of the Cockatiel with the cockatoos seems justified. Because of its exterior appearance, however, it holds a special position, and for this reason it is set apart from the true cockatoos as a separate group. Many behavior patterns are, in quality as in quantity, identical to those of the cockatoos, but a single developmental trend is not clearly evident. It appears to be more a development in different directions, in which *Nymphicus* underwent the greatest change in body shape. This may be considered an adaptation to the living conditions in central Australia and so a convergence with the corresponding characters of the broad-tailed parakeets. In behavior *N. hollandicus* differs too fundamentally to justify classification with them.

Bibliography

Barett, C. 1949. *Parrots of Australia*. Jersey City, NJ.

Bedford, 12th Duke of. 1969. *Parrots and Parrot-like Birds*. Neptune, NJ: T.F.H. Publications.

Berndt, R., and Meise, W. 1966. *Naturgeschichte der Vögel*. Stuttgart.

Boetticher, H. v. 1943. Gedanken über die systematische Stellung einiger Papageien. *Zoologischer Anzeiger*, S. 191-200.

———. 1964. *Die Papageien* (3. Aufl.). Wittenberg.

Brereton, J. L. 1963. Evolution within the Psittaciformes. *Proc. XIIth Intl. Orn. Congr.*, pp. 499-517.

———. 1963. The Life Cycle of Three Australian Parrots. *The Living Bird*, Vol. 2, pp. 21-29.

———. 1971. Inter-animal Control of Space. In *Behavior and Environment*, pp. 69-91. New York.

Brereton, J. L., and Immelmann, K. 1962. Head-scratching in the Psittaciformes. *The Ibis*, 104, pp. 169-175.

Brehm, A. E. 1900. *Brehms Tierleben* (3. Aufl.), Bd. 5. Leipzig & Vienna.

Cayley, N. W. 1938. *Australian Parrots, Their Habits in Field and Aviary*. Sydney.

———. 1954. *What Bird is That?* Sydney & London.

Chrisholm, A. H. 1965. *Bird Wonders of Australia*. Sydney.

Condon, H. T. 1975. *Checklist of the Birds of Australia*. Melbourne.

Dathe, H. 1974. *Handbuch des Vogelliebhabers*. Berlin.

Dorst, Jean. 1972. *Das Leben der Vögel*. [In English translation as *The Life of Birds*.]

Diercke, C. 1971. *Weltatlas* (160. Aufl.). Braunschweig.

Eastman, W. R., and Hunt, A. C. 1966. *The Parrots of Australia*. Sydney.

Eibl-Eibesfeld, I. 1972. *Liebe and Hass* (5. Aufl.). Munich.

———. 1974. *Grundriss der vergleichenden Verhaltensforschung* (4. Aufl.). Munich.

Forshaw, J. M. 1964. Some Field Observations on the Great Palm Cockatoo. *Emu* 63, pp. 327-331.

———. 1969, 1982. *Australian Parrots*. Melbourne.

———. 1973. *Parrots of the World*. Melbourne: Lansdowne Press; Neptune, NJ: T.F.H. Publications.

Finsch, O. 1868. *Die Papageien*, 2. Bd., 2. Hälfte. Leiden.

Grahl, W. de. 1973. *Papageien unserer Erde*, Bd. 1. Hamburg.

———. 1976. *Papageien in Haus und Garten*. Stuttgart. [In English translation as *The Parrot Family*.]

Hampe, H. 1935. Der Nymphensittich. *Vögel ferner Länder*, Bd. IX, Heft 4, S. 73ff. Braunschweig.

Hall, B. P. 1974. *Birds of the Harold Hall Australian Expeditions*. London.

Heidenreich, Manfred. 1982. Diseases of Parrots. In *Handbook of Lovebirds* by Horst Bielfeld, pp. 86-104. Neptune, NJ: T.F.H. Publications.

Immelmann, K. 1960. *Im unbekannten Australien*. Pfungstadt.

———. 1972. *Die Australischen Plattschweifsittiche* (3. Aufl.). Wittenberg-Lutherstadt. [In English translation as *Australian Parakeets*.]

Kolar, K. 1969. *Grzimeks Tierleben*, Bd. VIII, Zürich. [In English translation as *Grzimek's Animal Life*.]

Lendon, A. H. *Australian Birds in Captivity*. London.

Lorenz, K. 1965. *Der Kumpan in der Umwelt des Vogels*. Munich.

———. 1963. *Das sogenannte Böse, Zur Naturgeschichte der Aggression*. Vienna. [In English translation as *On Aggression*.]

Low, Rosemary. 1980. *Parrots, Their Care and Breeding*. London.

Neunzig, K. 1921. *Fremdländische Stubenvögel*. Magdeburg.

Nicholai, J. 1970. *Elternbeziehungen und Partnerwahl im Leben der Vögel*. Munich.

Peters, J. L. *Check-List of Birds of the World*, Vol. 3. Cambridge, MA.

Pinter, Helmut. 1979. *Handbuch der Papageienkunde*. Stuttgart.

Plath, K., and Davis, M. 1971. *This is the Parrot*. Neptune, NJ: T.F.H. Publications.

Reichenow, A. 1955. *Vogelbilder aus fernen Zonen* (2. Aufl.). Pfungstadt.

Russ, K. 1881. *Die Papageien*. Magdeburg.

Rutgers, A. 1969. *Die Sittiche und andere Papageien Australiens*. Gorssel.

Sabel, K. 1961. *Vogelfutterpflanzen*. Pfungstadt.

Serventy, D. L., and Whittell, H. M. 1967. *A Handbook of the Birds of Western Australia*. Perth.

Sharland, M. 1958. *Tasmanian Birds*. Sydney.

Smith, G. A. 1978. *Encyclopedia of Cockatiels*. Neptune, NJ: T.F.H. Publications.

Tembrock, G. 1964. *Verhaltensforschung* (2. Aufl.). Jena.

Thompson, D. W. 1900. On Characteristic Points in the Cranial Osteology of the Parrots. *Proc. Zool. Soc. London* (1899), pp. 9-46.

Wolters, H. E. 1975. *Die Vogelarten der Erde*. Hamburg.

**Male Gang-gang Cockatoo (*C. fimbriatum*)
resting. The filamentous feather crest
characteristic of this species shows well here.**

Red-vented Cockatoos (*C. haematuropygia*).

Indexes

Periodicals Utilized

Avicultural Magazine, Journal of the Avicultural Society, London.
Australian Aviculture. Melbourne, Australia.
AZ-Nachrichten, "Publication of the Central Exchange of the Registered Association of German Bird Breeders and Fanciers." Munich.
The Emu. Melbourne, Australia.
Die Gefiederte Welt, "Specialist Journal for Bird Fanciers and Breeders." Stuttgart.
Gefiederter Freund, "Official Publication of Exotis." Baar, Switzerland.
Geflügelbörse. Munich.
Magazine of the Parrot Society. Bedford, England.
Die Voliere, "the Specialist Newspaper for Bird Breeders, Keepers, and Fanciers." Hannover.
Zoonooz. San Diego, California.

Further reading on cockatoos from T.F.H. Publications:

Bates, Henry, and Busenbark, Robert. 1959, 1978. *Parrots and Related Birds.*
Decoteau, A. E. 1981. *Handbook of Cockatoos.*
Greene, W. T. 1884-87, 1979. *Parrots in Captivity.*
Nothaft, Ann. 1979. *Breeding Cockatoos.*
Teitler, Risa. 1980. *Taming and Training Cockatoos.*

Page numbers in boldface refer to illustrations.

Names

Included are English names not employed in this edition, but which elsewhere have been given to various cockatoos; these names are followed by "=" and the name used in this edition.

A

abbotti, see Lesser Sulphur-crested Cockatoo
Agapornis spp., 24
alba, see White Cockatoo
Alisterus spp., 40, 150
Amazona spp., 36, 52
assimilis, see Galah
aterrimus, see Palm Cockatoo

B

Banksian Cockatoo = Red-tailed Cockatoo
Bare-eyed Cockatoo = Little Corella
baudinii, see Black Cockatoo
Black Cockatoo (*Calyptorhynchus funereus*), 90-94, **90, 91**
Blue-eyed Cockatoo (*Cacatua ophthalmica*), 123-124, **123**
Budgerigar, 33, 36, 146, 147

C

Cacatua spp., 24, 28
Callocephalon, see Gang-gang Cockatoo
Calyptorhynchus spp., 24, 25, 28, 36, 40, 45, 58
citrinocristata, see Lesser Sulphur-crested Cockatoo
Citron-crested Cockatoo = Lesser Sulphur-crested Cockatoo *C. s. citrinocristata*
Cockatiel (*Nymphicus hollandicus*), 28, 29, 33, 36, 40, 44, 49, 81, 110, 145-152, **146, 150, 151**

D

djampeana, see Lesser Sulphur-crested Cockatoo
ducorpsii, see Ducorps's Cockatoo
Ducorps's Cockatoo (*Cacatua ducorpsii*), 144, **35, 70, 143**

E

eleonora, see Sulphur-crested Cockatoo
Eolophus, see Galah

F

fimbriatum, see Gang-gang Cockatoo
fitzroyi, see Sulphur-crested Cockatoo
funereus, see Black Cockatoo
Funereal Cockatoo = Black Cockatoo

G

Galah (*Eolophus rosecapillus*), 24, 28, 29, 32, 33, 36, 40, 41, 50, 58, 64, 77, 80, 105-110, 137, 138, 146, **11, 26, 27, 34, 35, 39, 67, 106, 107, 110**
Galapagos finches, 28
galerita, see Sulphur-crested Cockatoo
Gang-gang Cockatoo (*Callocephalon fimbriatum*), 24, 28, 60, 101-105, 110, 132, **102, 103, 154**
Glossy Cockatoo (*Calyptorhynchus lathami*), 99-101, **99**
goffini, see Goffin's Cockatoo
Goffin's Cockatoo (*Cacatua goffini*), 134-137, **78, 134, 135**
goliath, see Palm Cockatoo
Greater Sulphur-crested Cockatoo = Sulphur-crested Cockatoo
Grey Parrot, 36, 52
Ground Parrot, 77

H

haematuropygia, see Red-vented Cockatoo
hollandicus, see Cockatiel
Hooded Parakeet, 25

K

Kakapo, 12

L

lathami, see Glossy Cockatoo
latirostris, see Black Cockatoo
leadbeateri, see Major Mitchell's
  Cockatoo
Leadbeater's Cockatoo = Major
  Mitchell's Cockatoo
Lesser Sulphur-crested Cockatoo
  (*Cacatua sulphurea*), 29, 41, 110,
  114-117, 150, **frontis, 14, 15, 43,
  114, 115**
Little Corella (*Cacatua sanguinea*),
  29, 32, 33, 41, 108, 110, 137-141,
  146, **18, 22, 31, 38, 42, 78, 138**
Long-billed Corella (*Cacatua
  tenuirostris*), 16, 25, 141-143, **142**

M

macrorhynchus, see Red-tailed
  Cockatoo
magnificus, see Red-tailed Cockatoo
Major Mitchell's Cockatoo (*Cacatua
  leadbeateri*), 41, 44, 108, 110, 111-
  113, 133, **23, 42, 46, 67, 71, 111,
  122**
Moluccan Cockatoo = Salmon-
  crested Cockatoo
moluccensis, see Salmon-crested
  Cockatoo
mollis, see Major Mitchell's Cockatoo
Monk Parakeet, 21, 77

N

naso, see Red-tailed Cockatoo
Neophema spp., 33, 145
Night Parrot, 12, 33
normantoni, see Little Corella
Nymphicus, see Cockatiel

O

occidentalis, see Lesser Sulphur-
  crested Cockatoo
ophthalmica, see Blue-eyed Cockatoo

P

Palm Cockatoo (*Probosciger aterrimus*),
  24, 32, 41, 45, 53, 80, 85-90, **6,
  30, 86, 159**
parvula, see Lesser Sulphur-crested
  Cockatoo
pastinator, see Long-billed Corella
Pink Cockatoo = Major Mitchell's
  Cockatoo
Platycercus spp., 25, 40, 145, 150-152

Plum-crowned Parrot, 129
Polytelis spp., 33, 145
Probosciger, see Palm Cockatoo

Q

Quarrion = Cockatiel

R

Red-tailed Cockatoo (*Calyptorhynchus
  magnificus*), 94-99, 150, **30, 34, 47,
  94, 98**
Red-vented Cockatoo (*Cacatua
  haematuropygia*), 132-134, **131, 155**
Red-winged Parrot, 40
Roseate Cockatoo = Galah
Rose-breasted Cockatoo = Galah
roseicapillus, see Galah
Rosellas, see *Platycercus* spp.

S

Salmon-crested Cockatoo (*Cacatua
  moluccensis*), 33, 41, 49, 52, 55, 58,
  87, 124-128, **66, 126, 127**
sanguinea, see Little Corella
samueli, see Red-tailed Cockatoo
Slender-billed Cockatoo = Long-
  billed Corella
stenolophus, see Palm Cockatoo
Sulphur-crested Cockatoo (*Cacatua
  galerita*), 32, 41, 53, 87, 108, 110,
  118-122, 139, **7, 10, 31, 70, 75,
  82, 83, 118, 122**
sulphurea, see Lesser Sulphur-crested
  Cockatoo

T

tenuirostris, see Long-billed Corella
triton, see Sulphur-crested Cockatoo

U

Umbrella Cockatoo = White
  Cockatoo

W

White Cockatoo (*Cacatua alba*), 33,
  36, 41, 48, 53, 58, 87, 128-131,
  19, 74, 75, 79, 130, 158
White-tailed Cockatoo = Black
  Cockatoo C. f. baudinii

Y

Yellow-tailed Cockatoo = Black
  Cockatoo C. f. funereus

Subjects

A

Acclimation, 51, 73, 88, 93
Age, 21, 50, 116
Aggression, 77, 113, 133, 142-144
Agonistic behavior, 44, 87, 112, 116,
  129, 152, **30, 31, 78, 91**
Animal foods, 64-65, 86, 92, 93, 96,
  100, 104, 108, 120, 139
Artificial rearing, 82, 97
Aviaries, 56-59

B

Bathing, 40, 56-58, 68, 77
Beak, 12, 16, 25, 44, 52-59, 60, 69,
  77, 86, 92, 96, 109, 110, 125, 129,
  136, 140, 150
Biting, 88, 129
Breeding season, 32-33, 77, 88, 92-
  93, 96, 100, 104, 108, 112, 116,
  120, 124, 128, 136, 139, 146

C

Cages, 52, 116, **49, 51, 53**
Cage situation, 54, 69
Cavity breeding, 21, 32, 76-77
Cere, 28
Chaining, 55
CITES, *see* Washington Convention
Classification, *see* Systematics
Claw trimming, 54, 69
Climbing, 52-56
Clutch size, 80, 93, 108, 112, 116,
  120, 124, 125, 128, 132, 140, 141,
  148
Coloration, 20, 25, 110, 148, 150
Convergent evolution, 24, 137, 152
Copulation, 45, 76, 80, 148, 152
Courtship, 44, 93, 96, 108, 112, 117,
  128, 148, **47**
Crest, 24, 110
Crop, 16, 100

D

Development of young, 21, 89, 98,
  105, 121-122, 128, 141, 149, **14,
  15, 82, 83, 135**
Diastaxis, 20
Digestive organs, **17**
Distribution, 8, 60, 110, 145, **9**
Domestication, 76
Drinking behavior, 36, 146

Young White Cockatoo (*C. alba*) stretching, showing the yellow on the underside of the wing.

Palm Cockatoo, *Probosciger aterrimus*.

E

Ear patches, 25
Endangered species, 8, 49, 86, 92, 99, 112, 136
Endoscopy, 89

F

Feathering, 20, 50-51, 68, 132, 150, **20**
Feather lice, 21
Feather plucking, 60, 104, 127, 131
Feather trimming, 52, 55, 68-69, 72, 77, 133
Feeding behavior, 29, 36, 108, 141-142, 150, **35, 38, 66, 67, 98**
Feeding utensils, 54-56, 69
Feeding young, 45, 81, 148-149, 152, **42**
Fleeing, 40, 41
Flights, 58
Flocking behavior, 24, 29-32, 85, 92, 96, 100, 102, 106, 112, 115, 119, 132, 137, 141, 144, 145
Flying ability, 25, 36, 52, **18, 30, 39, 110**
Food, 16, 32-33, 60-66, 77, 86, 88, 92, 93, 96, 97, 100-101, 104-105, 108-109, 112-113, 117, 120-121, 124-126, 129, 131, 133, 136, 139, 140, 141, 142-143, 148
Foot, 12, 15, 21, 36, 40
Fostering, 110
Fruits, 64
Fungus infestation, 63, 89

G

Gnawing, *see* Beak
Green foods, 64
Grooming, 37, 41, 68, 72-73, 76, 152, **27, 38, 150**

H

Habitat, **10, 31, 87, 95, 119, 139, 147**
Hand-rearing, *see* Artificial rearing
Health, signs of, 49-50, 88, 133
Hybridization, 105, 106, 110, 133, 140
Hygiene, 69

I

Illness, 72, 108, 132-133

Incubation, 43, 45, 80, 88-89, 97, 100, 104, 105, 108, 110, 112, 116, 120-121, 124, 125, 130, 132, 133, 136-137, 140-141, 143, 148, 152
Individual distance, 32, 40
Intelligence, 49

L

Lighting, 56-59, 117
Locomotion, 36

M

Mate feeding, 41-43, 92, 152
Maturation, 24, 29, 50, 76, 132
Minerals, 65
Mites, 53
Monogamy, 24, 76
Muscles, 16

N

Nest boxes, 56, 77, 89-90, 98, 105, 109, 113, 117, 121, 124, 127, 130-131, 133, 136-137, 143, 148
Nest helpers, 97
Nesting density, 32, 146
Nesting materials, 78-79
Nestling period, 21, 80, 88-89, 97, 98, 101, 104, 105, 109-110, 112, 116, 120-121, 124, 129-131, 133, 137, 140, 143, 148
Nest site, 88, 93, 97, 100, 104, 108, 112, 125, 140, 146, 148, **27, 39, 42, 67, 71, 78, 107**
Newspaper, 53
Nomadism, 29, 92, 96, 120, 137, 144-145
Nutritional specialization, 60, 88, 101, 104

O

Oil gland, 20

P

Pair bonding, 24, 29, 41-44, 76, 121
Peck order, 112
Perches, 54-56, 69
Polishing, 32, 108, 137
Preening, 41, 44, 76, **70**
Protein requirements, 61, 64-65, 105
Plumage, *see* Feathering

Q

Quarantine, 16, 50

R

Ritualized behavior, 41, 44
Rumination, 100

S

Sand, 16, 53, 65, 69
Scratching, 40, 72
Seeds, 60-63
Selective advantage, 28
Sentinels, 29, 32, 92, 108, 120
Sexual dimorphism, 20, 50, 76, 89, 98, 101, 148, 150
Shelter, 59
Singly-kept pets, 48-49, 52, 72-73, 124, 142
Skeletal structure, 12, 28, 149-150, **13**
Sleeping, 37
Social behavior, 24, 29, 40-45, 48, 72-73, 120
Sprouts, 62-63
Stands, 54-55, **55, 57**
Stretching, 17, **35, 155**
Systematics, 12, 24, 28, 40, 99, 105, 110, 137, 149-152

T

Tail structure, 25
Talking, 49, 97, 104, 109
Tameness, 48, 55, 68, 72-73, 104, 109, 112, 113, 116, 120, 125, 129, 136, 142, 147
Temperature, 37, 51, 58-59, 69, 104, 116
Transport, 50
Tongue, 16, 36, 60, 86
Topography, **84**

V

Variety in diet, 61, 66, 77, 81
Vegetables, 64
Vitamins, 63, 65-66, 77

W

Washington Convention, 89, 104, 109, 116
Water, 69, 109
Wing trimming, *see* Feather trimming
Wings, 25
Wire mesh, 58, 126, 129